ACCIDENTS IN NORTH AMERICAN MOUNTAINEERING

VOLUME 8 • NUMBER 4 • ISSUE 57

2004

THE AMERICAN ALPINE CLUB
GOLDEN

THE ALPINE CLUB OF CANADA
BANFF

ISSN   0065-082X

ISBN   0-930410-96-3
Manufactured in the United States

Published by
The American Alpine Club, Inc.
710 Tenth Street, Suite 100
Golden, CO 80401

Cover Illustrations
Front: Following a lightning strike, Rangers Jack McConnell and Marty Vidak prepare to haul injured climber Rodrigo Liberal up the Friction Pitch on the Exum Ridge route on the Grand Teton. Photograph by Leo Larson—Grand Teton National Park.

Back: Johnson Canyon, near Banff in Canada. "Someone was climbing and became unattached from the ice tool—and just left it there. Someone else had to rap down and get it for him." Photograph by Al Hospers. *(Editor's Note: An appropriate caption might be, "To leash or not to leash, that is the question.")*

 Printed on recycled paper

CONTENTS

SAFETY COMMITTEES 2003

The American Alpine Club

Aram Attarian, John Dill, Mike Gauthier, Renny Jackson,
Daryl Miller, Jeff Sheetz, and John E. (Jed) Williamson *(Chair)*

The Alpine Club of Canada

Helmut Microys, Peter Amann, Peter Roginski,
Simon Ruel, Murray Toft *(Chair)*

ACCIDENTS IN
NORTH AMERICAN MOUNTAINEERING
Fifty-Seventh Annual Report of the Safety Committees

This is the fifty-seventh issue of Accidents in North American Mountaineering and the twenty-sixth issue in which The Alpine Club of Canada has contributed data and narratives.

Canada: This was the year of the avalanche. In two incidents involving backcountry skiers 14 people died. Although these incidents did not involve climbers, the effect will be felt by the climbing community for years to come. Parks Canada is currently revising their rules to require "custodial" groups (the definition of which is possibly as wide as "minors not accompanied by their parents") to hire professional guides to accompany them into the Park areas. This is a major change in philosophy and noteworthy for that reason alone.

It was also the year of the falling object. Spontaneous or climber-generated rock fall, ice fall, or hold failure accounted for a remarkably high number of incidents, resulting in a variety of injuries. Also of note this year was the unusually difficult forest fire situation which forced the closure of many areas in the National and Provincial Parks in Alberta and British Columbia in late July and August. Despite this fact, an increased number of accidents were reported this year.

Once again, it was difficult to get accident data from outside of the Rockies. There are many climbing areas in British Columbia, Ontario, and Quebec for which we have no data. If anyone has knowledge of a climbing or mountaineering accident, please report it to the editor. You may be able to help others avoid a similar fate in a similar situation.

We would like to express our gratitude to the following individuals who contributed to the Canadian section of this year's book: John Booth, Burke Duncan, Stephane Durocher, Jonathan Holzman, Brent Kozachenko, Mike Lezarre, Jim Mamalis, George Porter, Dave Stephens and Bradford White. Thanks also to those who indicated that they had nothing to report this year and to those whose reports were not included in this year's book.

United States: The number of accidents submitted for this year was significantly lower when compared to the last two decades. Even with three of the high-traffic climbing places—Rocky Mountain National Park, Joshua Tree National Park, and Devil's Lake State Park—not forwarding reports, this is important to consider when we know that climbing activity in the U.S. has increased. I stand by the estimate of about 300,000 climbers (people who rope up ten days or more a year), so when we look at the ratio of the number of accidents and fatalities to the number of climbers, it is hard to understand how the sport gets ranked by the National Safety Council as being in the top five in terms of risk level.

Under the category "falling rock, ice, or object," all eleven incidents this year were the result of rocks being dislodged, either by foot or by hand. In only two cases could this have been attributed to a failure to test holds. The primary reason was being in areas known for loose rock. Several narratives are devoted to this topic.

For many years I have been saying that we seem to be past the problem of rappelling off the end of the rope. But there have been several of these in the past few years. I am told that with the use of longer ropes, some climbers are reluctant to tie the rope-ends together for fear the knot will get hung up when the ropes are thrown down. I guess it depends on which of the two situations you would prefer to be exposed to.

Most of the descending errors this year were the result of lowering climbers—both from the bottom (sling-shot belays) and the top—rather than rappels. These were primarily due to ropes being too short (and no knot being tied in the end), speed build-up so the belayer could not hang on, and inadequate anchoring.

For the sake of continuity, we have used the original format for Table III, with a few minor changes—such as removing the word "bad" in front of weather. I have developed a matrix (first designed by Dan Meyer) of potential accident causes that has three major headings: unsafe conditions, unsafe acts, and errors in judgment. Table III does not include such descriptors as "physical and/or psychological profile," "trying to stick to a schedule," and "trying to please other people." When analyzing an accident, it is important to look at the variety of ways that climbers interact with the climbing environment, their partners, and the equipment they have chosen. For those interested in the topic, consider attending the annual Wilderness Risk Managers Conference, this year to be held in Banff from October 28 to 30. (Go to www.NOLS.org for information.)

In addition to the dedicated individuals on the Safety Committee, we are grateful to the following—with apologies for any omissions—for collecting data and helping with the report: Hank Alicandri, Micki Canfield, Dave Brown, Al Hospers, Tom Moyer, Steve Muelhauser, Leo Paik, Steve Rollins, Brad Shilling, Robert Speik, Eric White, all individuals who sent in personal stories, and, of course, George Sainsbury.

John E. (Jed) Williamson
Managing Editor
7 River Ridge Road
Hanover, NH 03755
e-mail: jedwmsn@sover.net

Edwina Podemski
Canadian Editor
700 Phipps McKinnon Building
10020-101A Avenue
Edmonton, Alberta T5J 3G2
e-mail: cwep@compusmart.ab.ca

CANADA

AVALANCHE
Alberta, Banff National Park, Mount Wilson, Wilson Major
On January 10, J.W. (29) and J.S. (23) were approaching the ice climb Wilson Major on Mount Wilson. They had climbed up the WI III approach pitches of Lady Wilson's Cleavage and were traversing the steep snow slopes below Wilson Major when they triggered a slab avalanche and were swept down into the trees below. Neither was totally buried, but J.S. suffered a broken ankle from impact with a tree. J.W. wrapped J.S. up in blankets and descended to the Saskatchewan Crossing Warden Station where the district warden's wife was able to call for a Warden rescue team. J.S. was evacuated by heli-sling to a waiting ambulance.

Analysis
Avalanches are one of the major objective dangers to ice climbing in the Rockies. On some climbs the danger is just from avalanches sweeping down the waterfall from terrain above, but in many instances there are avalanche slopes that need to be crossed on the approach or descent route or on low angle sections that hold snow on the climb itself. There are numerous cases of ice climbing parties being involved in avalanches that they themselves triggered. It is not uncommon for ice climbers to travel without avalanche rescue gear such as beacons probes and shovels. In this instance the party triggered a slab on an early season deep instability of facets on crust. The weakness was well known throughout the ranges of Canada in the winter of 2003 and was the layer attributed to most of the fatal avalanches that occurred. It is not known what level of avalanche awareness the party had or if they were cognizant of the avalanche danger rating of "Considerable" in the area. This party was very fortunate that they did not suffer more serious injuries as the avalanche ran down over small cliffs and into mature timber. If there had been a total burial, neither had the gear to perform a self-rescue. It is common practice in avalanche terrain for one person to cross a suspect slope at a time while the other observes from an island of safety. (Source: Parks Canada Warden Service, Bradford White)
(Editor's Note: With skiers included, there have been 70 avalanche fatalities within the past five years.)

FALL ON ICE
Alberta, Banff National Park, Five Mile Creek, Mount Cory, Dumber
On January 19, D.B. and G.H. were top-roping an ice climb known as "Dumber" above Five Mile Creek on the east slopes of Mount Cory. While attempting to step up on his crampon after placing his tools, G.H.'s foot slipped and he smashed his knee against the ice and dislocated his kneecap. D.B. tied G.H. off and also placed an ice screw under each foot to ease the strain of hanging, he then descended to call for help from a place where

he could get cell reception. Wardens responded to the scene by HFRS (Helicopter Flight Rescue System), splinted the leg and lowered G.H. to a point where he could be packaged on a vacuum mattress, stretcher and Baumann bag and heli-slung out.

Analysis

Top-roping does not necessarily mean that a slip may not cause an injury, as this incident points out. It is important to be sure that one's tool or crampon placement is secure before placing full weight on it. It is not known why D.B. did not lower G.H. further down to a point where he would not have been hanging. (Source: Parks Canada Warden Service, Bradford White)

FALL ON ICE, PROTECTION (TOOLS) PULLED
Alberta, Banff National Park, Mount Murchison, Balfour Wall

On February 9, R.C. (40) was with a large group climbing on the Balfour Wall, an area with a variety of one-pitch top-ropeable ice climbs on the lower slopes of Mount Murchison in Banff National Park. R.C. was about half way up a pitch that he was leading and had stopped to place his first screw. His tools pulled out and he fell down to the base of the pitch and broke both of his ankles. Part of the team descended to the Icefields Parkway where they flagged down a passing Parks vehicle and reported the accident. A warden rescue team heli-slung into the site, splinted both ankles, and R.C. was heli-slung out to a waiting ambulance.

Analysis

Broken lower limbs are the most common injury in ice climbing falls. It is also fairly common to break both legs/ankles. The only real way to prevent such injuries while ice climbing is not to fall. (Source: Parks Canada Warden Service, Bradford White)

FALL ON ICE, UNROPED
Alberta, Banff National Park, Johnston Canyon

On February 13, L.R. (26) and her boyfriend (L.) were doing some ice climbing at the upper falls in Johnston Canyon, a popular area of one pitch top-ropeable ice climbs. L.R. unclipped from the belay station, which was about ten meters up some low-angle ice from the canyon bottom, and climbed down to her pack to get some water. On the climb back up to the stance she slipped and fell back down to the bottom, catching her crampon and breaking her ankle and lower leg in the process. Passers by descended to the phone at the bottom of the trail and called the Warden Service to report the accident. Meanwhile L. fashioned an improvised splint from ice tools and a jacket and began to piggy-back carry L.R. down the trail. A rescue crew of wardens and paramedics met the pair part way, re-splinted the leg, administered morphine for the pain and wheeled the patient down to the ambulance in the wheeled stretcher.

Analysis

It is unlikely that most parties would have belayed on the low angle ice where L.R. fell, but this incident shows the possible consequences of even a simple slip in low-angle terrain. While L. showed his self-reliance capabilities in this case by improvising a splint and beginning a self-rescue, L.R.'s lower leg was quite badly broken, the splint did not immobilize the knee, and she was in considerable discomfort while being carried. In a location like this where rescue response was close by it would have been a better choice of action to have made the patient warm and comfortable and wait for a rescue team rather than risk further complications to the leg injury. (Source: Parks Canada Warden Service, Bradford White)

FALL ON ROCK, CLIMBING ALONE AND UNROPED
Alberta, Kananaskis Country, Mount Lorette, South Ridge

On February 17, A.S. (18) set out to make a solo climb of Mount Lorette's South Ridge (5.6). His family became concerned when he did not return home later that evening as scheduled. His body was discovered about 120 meters from the summit near the southeast ridge of Mount Lorette the following morning. Measuring from where rescue specialists found marks on the slope and from the apparent trajectory, it appeared that he fell while doing the hand traverse about halfway up the climb and had fallen approximately 400 feet to his death. When found, he was wearing a helmet and harness, and was tied into the end of a climbing rope.

Analysis

George Field, public safety specialist for Kananaskis Country, indicates that this is not usually a tough climb, but, "Soloing is definitely raising the danger factor," he said. The area where A.S. was found is a popular place for climbers and there hasn't been a fatality in the 19 years Field has worked in the area. "But in the winter with snow and the loose rock, you're taking a chance," Field said. (Source: Canada.com, Mike D'Amour, *Calgary Sun*)

FALLING ICE
Alberta, Banff National Park, Lake Louise, Louise Falls

On February 22, an ice climber at Louise Falls was injured in an accident similar to a fatal mishap that occurred a year ago at the same location. He was climbing solo and using a device to belay himself. The climber had completed the first pitch at the time of the accident. A 15 by 20-foot piece of ice broke apart from the icefall 50 feet above. Upon hearing the ice crash, the man dived for his nearest anchor and was darted by a number of pieces of ice. The segment which hit him was the approximately the size of a soccer ball. Several people were in the area that afternoon and assisted him to the base of the climb. A person contacted the warden service by cell phone. Wardens responded by snowmobile. (Source: Geneviève Behara, *Banff Crag and Canyon*)

Analysis

As we know, whenever there is a rapid and significant change in temperatures, ice responds by contracting or expanding. When the weather becomes colder, ice first expands and so is more likely to crack. The weather had been fairly mild until a sudden cold snap in the week before the incident.

AVALANCHE, CLIMBING ALONE
Alberta, Canmore, Mount Lady MacDonald

On or about March 13, J.F (20) decided to make a solo scramble towards the summit of Mount Lady MacDonald. He was not one to follow the regular path and likely ascended directly toward the summit on the left side of an obvious gully on the West Face. Avalanche bulletins from around that date indicate that avalanche danger was considered "Extreme."

On June 7, the body of J.F. was recovered by Canmore RCMP from the gully. Hikers in the area reported finding the body. The deceased was in a face down, prone position lying across the fall line with his rubber boots still on. There was a column of snow around his upper arm and the remainder of the debris was flat with rocks embedded along the flanks. These visual clues led investigators to believe that he had been involved in an avalanche accident. The medical examiner's office indicated that J.F. likely died from suffocation consistent with an avalanche. It is speculated that the victim left the summit ridge and crossed into a bowl area near the top of the gully, where he was caught in an avalanche, slid down the gully to below the teahouse level, and was buried in avalanche debris until the warmer temperatures uncovered him. (Source: *Canmore Leader*, Burke Duncan, George Field)

Analysis

Although this is not a climbing accident and thus not included in the data, it is illustrative of the problems which can occur when hiking or climbing alone. There was no one there to attempt to rescue him when the avalanche occurred and his family and friends were unaware of his fate for three months, as no one knew where to begin the search.

Leave the following with a friend: your plans and time line, specific route(s) you plan to try, vehicle description and license number, gear description, and who/when to call and your cell phone number if you plan to carry one. If you plan to hike or climb solo, recognize that this increases the risk. Check for the current weather and avalanche conditions. It should go without saying that one should not climb or ski in avalanche terrain when the avalanche danger is posted "Extreme."

FALL ON ROCK, FAILURE TO TEST HOLDS, PROTECTION PULLED OUT
Alberta, Bow Valley, Yamnuska, CMC Wall

On June 15, a female climber was leading on the CMC Wall on Yamnuska (Mount John Laurie). On the third pitch near the top, she pulled out some large loose rocks. She fell approximately 15 meters, pulling out an old fixed pin, but was held by a bolt. Her partner, a certified mountain guide, called 911 for assistance and lowered her to the bottom of the climb. She was then evacuated by helicopter. The climber suffered a dislocated left knee and pain in her right ankle.

Analysis

The Yamnuska crag has been described by some as "a hopeless pile of garbage rock." The significant effect of freeze-thaw cycles is evident in the large scree slopes below the cliff face. There is plenty of good rock to be found on the crag, but it is important to test holds before committing to them.

FALL ON ROCK, CLIMBING ALONE AND UNROPED
Alberta, Kananaskis Country, Mount Lorette

On July 15, a 23-year-old man, who had set out on a solo climb of Mount Lorette's South Ridge (5.6), failed to return home as expected. He left a note describing the planned route and expected return time. A search was mounted by Kananaskis RCMP, Canmore and Kananaskis conservation officers, Alpine Helicopters and supported by Kananaskis Emergency Medical Services. "Searchers flew around the area and they found what they thought was a backpack and when they went down for a closer look they confirmed that it was the climber," said Kananaskis EMS spokesman Rob Jones. The unidentified climber was found at the foot of a scree slope. It appears that he lost his grip or footing and had fallen down the slope for approximately 150 to 200 feet. (Source: Pablo Fernandez, *Calgary Sun*)

FALL ON ROCK
Alberta, Banff National Park, Moraine Lake, Schiesser Ledges Route

On July 23, G.A. (62) was a member of a guided party that was on a multi-day traverse in the ten peaks area in Banff National Park. The party had climbed up to The Neil Colgan Hut from the Fay Hut and had spent two days ascending peaks in the vicinity of the hut. On the day of the accident, they had descended from the hut down the Schiesser Ledges route and had finished all of the down-climbing and rappels. They had unroped and taken off their harnesses and helmets and were walking down the moraine towards Moraine Lake when G.A. fell off the side of the moraine and tumbled about 50 meters down the steep side wall. The guide quickly climbed down to him and found him unconscious from a head injury and facial trauma. One of the members of the party used the handheld radio that the group carried and began transmitting "Mayday!" over the Park's frequency. Eventually dispatchers and rescue crews were able to make two-way contact with the reporting person and determine where the accident had taken place. G.A. was heli-slung from the site by HRFS and transported by Air and Stars Air Ambulance to Calgary.

G.A. spent two weeks in hospital and had full expectation of recovery from his injuries, but shortly after he was transferred from the ICU, he developed blood clots and subsequently died.

Analysis

In the kind of terrain where G.A. fell, most anybody would walk comfortably unroped. The top of the moraine at that point was several meters wide. G.A. had spent several days previously in much more technical terrain and according to the guide had demonstrated surefootedness and a good tolerance for exposure. There is conjecture that G.A. may have suffered some loss of consciousness before his fall, but he could not remember any of the details of the incident and none of the party witnessed the events prior to seeing him actually falling down the side of the slope. It is good practice for guides to teach guests how to operate the two-way radios they carry and instruct them on what information to relay if they have to call in for assistance. A clear description of the problem and the exact location of the incident are the most important to rescue crews.

A sad footnote to this story is the fact that G.A.'s wife had died two years previously on a guided ski trip in the Alps and this trip was G.A.'s first return to the mountains since that incident. (Source: Parks Canada Warden Service, Bradford White)

FALLING ROCK, FALL ON ROCK
Alberta, Jasper National Park, Throne Mountain

On August 16, an experienced party of five were climbing the notched northeast ridge of Throne Mountain. After reaching the summit, the group was descending, mostly unroped, in third class terrain. At one of the notches, three members of the group were awaiting their turn to tie into the ropes and ascend when one of the leading members dislodged a rock. P.K. dodged the rock but lost his footing and fell for at least 100 meters down broken ledges, finally coming to rest in an ice filled gully. A marginal emergency call was made by cell phone to the park dispatch and rescue team was notified. One member of the party rappelled down the face and located the fallen climber, seriously injured but alive. Parks Canada rescue teams evacuated P.K. and the rest of the party by helicopter in failing light.

P.K. suffered a serious head injury, a variety of non-serious fractures and massive bruising. At the date of publication, he has made a largely successful recovery from these injuries.

Analysis

When climbing and scrambling in easy alpine terrain, loose rock is always a major consideration. This party's ability to communicate with emergency responders undoubtedly saved the life of P.K., who likely would not have survived the night out on the mountain. (Source: Parks Canada Warden Service, Jim Mamalis, John Booth)

FALLING ROCK
Alberta, Jasper National Park, Mount Fryatt

In the early morning of August 29, a party of four left their bivouac site in the Geraldine Lakes drainage to climb the southwest face of Mount Fryatt (3661 meters). The night had been clear and there was a frost in the alpine which had coated the rocks making them slippery. At 1400 they stopped at approximately 3,140 meters to put their crampons on in order to cross a small section of snow and ice. As they were putting on their crampons, rockfall from the terrain above struck R.S. on the back of the helmet. She was knocked unconscious with enough force to crack her helmet and lacerate her scalp. The terrain at their position on the upper part of the southwest face was low fourth class with few sheltered locations.

The group secured J.S. and compressed the wound on her head while she regained consciousness. Then they contacted the Jasper National Park Warden Service with a satellite phone. J.S. was heli-slung off the mountain beneath a helicopter at 1,650. She was transferred to an ambulance at the road and driven to the Jasper hospital. By 1715 the rest of the party had been heli-slung from the face to the advanced staging area and then inside a helicopter to the road.

Analysis

Rock fall is a common danger on the big face routes of the Rockies and is often more common in alpine terrain during the hotter part of the day. The route was bathed in sunlight when the rock fall occurred. It may have been prudent for the group to have set themselves a turn-around time earlier in the day so that they could have been well away from the face at the time the rock fall occurred.

The group appeared to be experienced and well prepared. Having a satellite phone in their possession greatly expedited their evacuation. (Source: Parks Canada Warden Service, Jim Mamalis)

FALL ON ROCK–FOOTHOLD BROKE, PROTECTION PULLED OUT
Alberta, Jasper National Park, Tonquin Valley, Mount Oubliette

A.M. and I just got back from the Tonquin where (I believe) we did the first ascent of a direct start to the Beckey (East Ridge) Route on Mount Oubliette. The route was approximately 450 meters long and 5.9. We had intended to do the upper ridge, but it rained until well after our wake-up time. By 8:00 a.m. on August 29, the sun was out and drying things out quickly. We went to have a look at the direct, and before we knew it were well on our way. An initial wide crack up the lower slab and more low angle stuff led to the large left facing corner that is obvious in the Select Alpine Climbs guide picture. We followed this on generally good rock (though quite dirty in places) and avoided several roofs on the right. On the last technical pitch, A.M. took a huge lead fall when a lot of rock gave out under her weight, pulling her top piece. The fall came on the last pitch of 5th class, about 350 meters up the route. A.M. was up about 40 meters on what had been generally good rock, at an easy grade. She is a competent 5.10 trad leader, but without much new route experience. She started to encounter some blocky, loose looking rock and dodged some of it to the right, but then took on some more in a steep bit. Fearing its instability, she started to down-climb a bit onto something she thought would be stable with a downward force. This whole section (approximately 50 pounds) broke free and sent her on her way. Her top piece was a #0 (purple) T.U. which was placed in blocky rock. She is fairly certain it held for a fraction of a second and thought perhaps the rock falling on her was the extra force required to pull it. Having talked about the situation more afterwards, based on where the half way mark was in the rope, it was at least a 60-foot fall. A large nut, also in somewhat blocky rock, held the fall. The rope was a 70-meter 9.4 mm Beal, which fortunately sustained only minor damage just above her tie-in point. The impact of the fall badly bruised her buttocks and it was the falling rock that appears to have done most the damage to her right leg.

At the time, it seemed as though she had torn ligaments in the leg, since it would support no weight in a flexed position. I tried to evaluate her disposition where she ended up, but her movements and coherence quickly ruled out head and spine injuries. She was lowered to the belay. I took cover in a shallow corner when she yelled, "Falling!" and could hear the amount of rock coming down. I sustained minor second-degree rope burns on the inside of my right thumb, but was not hit by rock. Badly shaken and with a pretty much useless right leg, we reluctantly calculated that finishing up and then descending the normal approach climb to the Beckey would be easier/safer than ten rappels. With the help of T3s and a lot of guts, A.M. was able to slowly second this pitch and then the following 120 meters of mostly 3rd and 4th class to the base of the Beckey. A.M.'s descent to the base of the mountain and the very slow progress over boulder fields back to the camp at Surprise Point was awe inspiring. This involved crappy ledge traverses, lowers down couloirs (one through a water fall which soaked her), bollard rappels over questionable snow bridges, a lot of sliding over rock strewn glacier ice at 30 degrees, and even some piggy-backing. This lasted from about 7:30 p.m. until 3:45 a.m. (We did not have radios.) After the self-rescue back to camp, I went to the nearest lodge looking for horse service out of the area, but was put in touch with the wardens via satellite phone and they arrived only 45 minutes later. In the end, it turns out that the worst injuries were contusions caused presumably by the rock fall. One very nasty wound left a fairly deep opening that projected parallel to the skin's surface. It is better that it hit her than the rope! (Source: C.F., partner of A.M.)

FALL ON ROCK, INEXPERIENCE
Alberta, Banff National Park, Cascade Mountain

On August 30, N.P. (16), C.B. (18) and J.P. (17) left Calgary in the afternoon and drove to Banff to the base of Cascade Mountain. The three left their vehicle and started scrambling up the climbers' left of Cascade Waterfall. Both C.B. and J.P. had scrambled around the base of the waterfall before, and J. P. had some indoor climbing gym experience. They did not have a clear plan as to how high up they would go and carried no climbing gear, but N.P. later stated that they thought there was a route that would go up to the top of the waterfall. C.B. was carrying a guitar on his back. At about two-thirds up the height of the falls where the terrain gets into steeper cliffs, C.B. slipped and fell about 50 meters into a large crack where he sustained a severe head injury and became wedged. J.P. descended to get help while N.P. waited with the victim. A passerby with a cell phone called the Warden Service, who responded with a rescue helicopter and paramedics. The rescuers stabilized the patient, including intubation and oxygen, and he was heli-slung directly from the incident site to the Mineral Springs Hospital where he died of his injuries.

Analysis

While not a climbing situation, this case illustrates many of the factors that are common in scrambling accidents: The persons involved were young males and even though one had some climbing gym experience, together they had little or no experience climbing in the mountains. They had not researched or planned their route or discussed it with anyone. They picked an objective close to the town and easily accessible.

Local education programs targeted to new staff that include discussions about the hazards of scrambling and free distributions of detailed route descriptions of the easiest route up each of the most commonly ascended local mountains have been instituted to try and reduce the numbers of scrambling incidents. Banff wardens responded to three other incidents of stranded or stuck scramblers in 2003. (Source: Parks Canada Warden Service, Bradford White)

FALL ON ROCK, FAILURE TO FOLLOW ROUTE, PROTECTION PULLED OUT
Alberta, Ghost River area, Bonanza

On September 6, a party of three were climbing Bonanza, a 5.8 gear route located in the Ghost River area. About midway up the route the leader, J.I. (34), got off route and climbed into increasingly difficult terrain. He placed three pieces of protection before he fell. The uppermost piece, a nut, pulled out and the leader fell approximately 25-35 meters. He struck his head on the rock while falling and was stopped by his belayer at an elevation a few meters below the belay stance. His party managed to get him over to the sloping ledge near the belay stance. The victim was losing consciousness. A nearby party of two guides had witnessed the fall and climbed up to the belay to assist. Before long they began CPR.

Another witness descended to a point where he could get cell phone reception and called 911 and was transferred to Warden Dispatch. A first-party Warden rescue team flew into the scene and began to set up at the top of the route for a technical rock rescue while a second helicopter in the area for fire duty was dispatched to bring in paramedics and a second rescue team. The rescuer was lowered to the patient and the patient was secured in the Baumannn bag. Because of the steepness of the cliff it was not possible to directly extract the rescuer and patient from the accident location, so the main rescue line at the top of the cliff was attached to the HFRS (long line) system and the entire package was heli-slung to the valley bottom. Paramedics examined the patient and he was pronounced dead at the staging area.

Analysis

Even with a guidebook, route finding on limestone is sometimes very tricky and often an easier looking section that is off route turns out to be more difficult and the climbing may also be loose and very difficult to protect.

The group had a discussion about where the route went from the belay and had come to a consensus that it must go up to the left when, in fact, a non-obvious traverse leads around the corner to the right. The leader was wearing a helmet at the time of the fall, but it was not enough to prevent a fatal injury. Had his last piece held, he may not have struck his head in the fall.

Cell phone coverage in the area is intermittent. It was fortunate for the party that they had a cell phone and managed to make contact, as it is 25 kilometers over rough gravel road to the nearest land line. (Source: Parks Canada Warden Service, Bradford White)

LATE START, FAILURE TO FOLLOW ROUTE, DARKNESS, STRANDED
Alberta, Kananaskis Country, Mount Indefatigable
On September 14, two women (28 and 36), from Canmore spent the night on a cliff ledge after darkness forced them to interrupt their climb of the Joy route on Mount Indefatigable. They left Canmore at about 9:00 a.m. and did not start their ascent of this lengthy route until late in the morning, at approximately 11:30 a.m. They finished it near dusk. The exit route they took was incorrect and put them on a series of cliffs. They reached a suitable bivvy ledge in the dark and elected to wait until first light to resume their exit. At first light, searchers found the climbers on this ledge and determined that they could not move up or down from their position. A helicopter dropped two conservation officers onto a cliff band above them. The women ascended to the conservation officers via a rope that was lowered to them and the group was then lifted to safety by the helicopter at about 11:30 a.m. September 15. Neither woman was hurt but both were cold and dehydrated. (Source: Cathy Ellis, Burke Duncan)
Analysis
The climbers later reported in the local news that they felt that they would have been able to complete their climb, but as the rescue team was already on hand, they elected to be helicoptered off the route. It should be noted that this was a high-risk evacuation for the pilot and rescuers due to very strong winds at all elevations.

FALL ON ROCK
Alberta, Banff National Park, Lake Louise, Back of the Lake Crag, Ash Wednesday
On October 10, T. (24) and his partner D., were climbing at the Back of the Lake crag area near Lake Louise. T. was leading the 10.b route Ash Wednesday when he fell and injured his ankle. His partner lowered him to the ground and T. attempted to hobble out but made it only as far as the lakeshore trail before he determined that the injury was more serious and painful than he first supposed. D. called for help on his cell phone. Warden rescuers splinted T.'s ankle and wheeled him out on a wheeled stretcher to a waiting ambulance. X-Rays determined that T. had a closed fracture of the left fibula.

Analysis
Lead falls even on well protected sport routes can result in injury. (Source: Parks Canada Warden Service, Bradford White)

FALL ON ROCK, PROTECTION PULLED OUT
Alberta, Banff National Park, Lake Louise, Back of the Lake Crag, Scared Peaches
On October 19, D.W. (24) was leading Scared Peaches, a 5.12a mixed-gear route on the Air Voyage Wall at the Back of the Lake Crag area in Lake Louise. He was several meters above the last protection that he had placed when he fell. The gear pulled and the result was a eight meter lead fall into a large boulder.

D.W. suffered a deep gash to the outside of his left thigh and was in considerable pain. His partner lowered him to the ground and one of the party ran down to report the incident. A team of warden rescuers packaged D.W. on site and he was moved with the help of the climbers in the area to a nearby open place where he could be evacuated by heli-sling to the waiting ambulance.

Analysis
It is unknown what type of gear D.W. had placed. Gear placements in the hard quartzite rock found at the Back of the Lake are normally quite good. Where natural gear is not possible, most routes have bolts. (Source: Parks Canada Warden Service, Bradford White)

FALLING ROCK
Alberta, Jasper National Park, Roche à Perdrix
On October 26, at 0700 J.H. (28) and M.L. (42) set out to climb the Diagonal Route on the west face of Roche à Perdrix. At 1100, they reached the summit and began a rappel down the Chimney Route on the North Ridge. The Chimney Route is equipped with rappel anchors and makes for a fast descent to the parking lot at the foot of the mountain. The team had two 60-meter ropes with them but used only one rope, as there were excessively high winds and they were concerned about getting their rappel lines stuck. After one 25-meter rappel, the two climbers met at a rappel station. J.H. tied the knots in the ends of the rope, threw the lines, and was about to commence the next rappel when he was struck in the head by a large free-falling rock. The impact drove him to his knees and left him unconscious. M.L. propped him up against the rock and checked for signs of life (which were present).

After approximately five minutes, J.H. regained consciousness, and returned to his feet. From this point, J.H. was able to move, though he was exhibiting a great deal of confusion. M.L. pulled the second rope out of his pack and used the two ropes together to lower J.H. down the remaining pitches in 50-meter lengths. After a very slow descent down the North Ridge, the climbers reached their car and went to the hospital. It was subsequently determined that J.H. had a concussion and a fractured vertebrae in his neck.

Analysis

The Chimney Route on Roche à Perdrix is a route that I have been on numerous times. The route is typically dry and rockfall is largely a rarity. For this reason, climbing strategies that are often applied to alpine routes with excessive rockfall dangers (winter ascents, climbing at night, etc.) are largely unnecessary. The fact that I was injured by rockfall on this route is, however, a strong testament to the fact that rockfall can occur anywhere and at anytime in the Canadian Rockies. For this reason, a good climbing helmet with the capability to absorb large top-impact forces is essential for alpine climbing. I survived this particular incident only because I was wearing a good helmet. (Source: J.H. and M.L.)

AVALANCHE, POOR POSITION, WEATHER
Alberta, Peter Lougheed Park, Mount Murray, R & D

On November 11, a party of ice climbers on the route R & D on Mount Murray in the Ranger Creek area, was hit by a size 1 to 1.5 avalanche before beginning the climb. One of the party had fallen after the avalanche had come to rest, breaking a bone in his left lower leg. A second size 1 to 1.5 avalanche struck the group as they moved towards safer ground.

Analysis

The local guidebook indicates that Ranger Creek is home to some of the earliest-formed ice. The area should, however, be avoided after heavy snow due to the surrounding avalanche terrain. On November 11, snow continued to fall heavily at the rate of one to two centimeters per hour during the course of the rescue and the roads were in poor condition. A ground evacuation was required. The terrain above the area was reloading, placing the party and all rescuers at risk during the 1.5 hour rescue. Given the conditions, perhaps the party should have avoided this area.

FALLING ICE–DISLODGED BY LEADER, POOR POSITION–BELAYER
Alberta, Banff National Park, Weeping Wall, Center Pillar

On December 21, J.R. (23) was belaying her husband who was leading up the second pitch of the Center Pillar area on the Weeping Wall in Banff National Park. The leader was about 30 meters above her when he dislodged a large piece of ice which hit J.R. directly on the head. The incident was witnessed by a party that was at the same level and about ten meters to the left of J.R. at the time.

T.D., who was with the witness party, described the incident on an internet message board: "The leader of the party was 30 meters above the belay when he dislodged a 20-30-pound plate of ice which fell directly onto his belayer's head. The impact was horrific and the belayer fell limp on the ice instantly. Within seconds she began to convulse/seize vigorously against the ice. After a brief discussion, my partner climbed quickly over to her stance to deliver any help that he could. Upon arrival at the belay my partner secured himself to the anchor and evaluated her. At first it appeared that she had suffered a fatal blow, but she made guttural noises that indicated an attempt at breathing. She was brought level, as she had slumped upside down. She then began to breathe on her own after her tongue was extracted from her airway.

"The leader at this point was obviously in shock, as his wife was near death, and he needed to be coached to build a multi-point anchor and begin rappelling to the belay. We determined that the victim was in need of immediate medical help and climbers at the base had already run for help. My partner and I arranged an assisted lower through the second belay down to the ground. At this time J.R. was semi-conscious and apparently stable. A 60-meter redirected lower to the ground was carried out. Climbers at the base had prepared a location for J.R. to be stabilized until rescue arrived. Wardens arrived on scene as the lower was completed and assumed control. A heli-sling operation was used to bring J.R. to an ambulance on the road where she was evaluated and then flown to Banff for treatment."

Analysis

The quick actions of the nearby party no doubt had a very significant bearing on the successful recovery of J.R. Their actions are to be commended. T.D. summed up his experience: "ALWAYS keep the belayer safe from falling ice. The leader had positioned his belay under his line of ascent. Don't risk your life or the lives of rescuers in an accident situation. Build extra anchors, add back-ups and be aware of loads on anchors. Rescues take time and eat up gear very quickly. Prusiks and locking 'biners are critical when managing lowers and raises. Speed is critical. The victim didn't breathe for three to four minutes before we got to her. The impact was at 11:00 a.m. and we had her lowered by 11:35 a.m. and in the helicopter by 12:30 a.m. (Source: internet message board: www.livethevision.com/wwwboard/messages/3636.html)

AVALANCHE
British Columbia, Selkirk Mountains North, Durrand Glacier

On January 20, a group of eleven backcountry skiers was caught in an avalanche. Three people were able to extricate themselves and they dug out one injured person. Seven other skiers perished from asphyxia. The avalanche was as much as 30 meters wide and 100 meters long. The bodies of the victims were buried under three to four meters of snow.

Analysis

As this is not strictly speaking, a ski mountaineering incident, the data is not included in the Tables. This report and the one which follows are included as they were the two most devastating alpine accidents in Canada in 2003.

The seeds of the January 20 avalanche were sown in November 2002 when a particularly unstable layer of snow was created at the beginning of a very unusual season. This layer had created problems throughout the season.

The avalanche hazards were rated as "Moderate" at the time of this incident. There was no evidence that the slide was triggered by the skiers and the ski party had not noticed any signs of concern. The avalanche bulletin for January 20 read as follows: "Changes to our snowpack have been occurring very slowly lately. With no significant snow to report in the last few days, our focus remains on the persistent instabilities found in the mid and lower snowpack. Surface hoar buried on Christmas Day now sits roughly 50-75 cm below the surface. This layer can be difficult to find and although strength tests indicate an improving trend, it remains a concern. Near the base of the snowpack a weak crust/facet combination from November persists. AVALANCHES: The frequency of avalanches observed has declined, but their size has not. Each day large avalanches continue to be reported in the Selkirks."

AVALANCHE
British Columbia, Glacier National Park, Mount Cheops
On February 1, a high school backcountry ski group comprised of three adults and 14 students was traveling on the Balu Pass Trail, about five kilometers west of the Rogers Pass summit. Parks Canada had warned that avalanches were possible in the higher alpine areas but were unlikely below the tree line, where the group was skiing. The group had been skiing about 15 meters apart, with one supervisor in front and the other two bringing up the rear. The skiers were halfway up the Connaught Creek Valley when the avalanche roared down the north face of Mount Cheops, burying the entire group. The slide began at a point between 2,200 to 2,300 vertical meters up Mount Cheops. It traveled for a kilometer and spread out 500 to 800 meters at the sides. The slide was so large it contained at least 1,000 tons of snow, according to information provided by the Canadian Avalanche Association. The toe of the slide ended at about the 1,500-meter elevation mark with parts of it more than five meters deep.

It is unlikely that this was a skier-triggered slide. Some of the skiers were buried as deep as three meters. The group was carrying the proper avalanche-rescue equipment, including personal locator beacons and shovels. Two professional guides happened to be nearby and were able to shout a warning and then come to the prompt assistance of the group. Unfortunately, there were seven fatalities.

Analysis
This tragedy was only about 30 kilometers away from the site of the smaller slide on January 20 (see above report).

This incident is of particular importance as it was instrumental in prompting the proposed changes to the Canadian National Parks regulations. Under the proposed regulations all "custodial groups" involving minors not accompanied by their parents (such as school or youth groups) will not be allowed into the backcountry without professional guides. At the time of the incident, avalanche danger above tree line was rated as "Considerable" but below tree line it was only rated as "Moderate."

FALL ON ROCK, INADEQUATE BELAY/ANCHOR
British Columbia, Squamish, Stawamus Chief, Exasperater
D.G. (41) fell 30 meters to his death while rock climbing on the Stawamus Chief on May 31. D.G. was an experienced climber who was roped into a harness at the time of his plunge from the Chief. D.G. had been climbing with a group on a section of the Chief's Grand Wall, known as Exasperater (5.10c). He was at the midway belay, approximately 100 feet off the ground when a second party asked him to rig a toprope for them. He complied, but during rigging somehow fell to the base of the granite monolith.

Emergency services including B.C. Ambulance Service, Squamish Fire and Rescue, and Squamish Search and Rescue were called out to the scene at about 5:30 p.m. Saturday. Attempts to resuscitate D.G. were unsuccessful. Paramedics temporarily revived him, but he died at the scene from massive head and chest injuries. (Source: Jane Seyd, *North Shore News*)

INADEQUATE ANCHOR AND BELAY
British Columbia, Bugaboo Glacier Provincial Park/Alpine Recreation Area, Snowpatch Spire
On July 18, a group of five climbers had climbed the Kraus/McCarthy Route on Snowpatch Spire. They were moving down to a rappel station and the victim (a sixty-four year old male) was down-climbing, belayed from above with his rope attached through a 'biner on a slung horn. The sling then popped off the horn and he fell approximately five meters and was stopped by his belayer. He dislocated the head of his upper arm. The group diagnosed the arm as being broken and a physician in the group provided first aid in the manner of immobilizing the arm. They then rappelled the route, assisting the injured man, and made their way back to the Conrad Kain Hut, where they called the air ambulance. The victim was flown to the Invermere Hospital and released the next day. The group handled the rescue very well and were totally self-sufficient until the guides took over at the hut. (Source: Dave Stark)

CLIMBING ALONE, DISAPPEARED, POSSIBLE FALL INTO CREVASSE
British Columbia, Mount Robson Provincial Park, Mount Robson
On July 31, L.B. (23) departed Berg Lake to climb Mount Robson's Fuhrer Ridge with a planned descent of the Kain Face. He failed to return as planned and a Parks Canada rescue team was notified. After two days of helicopter searching, a dog search of a natural avalanche and considerable investigative work, search efforts were suspended. No tracks or any other evidence were discovered on the mountain.
Analysis
The glaciated terrain on Mount Robson is riddled with crevasses and significant avalanche and icefall hazards exist. While search efforts for L.B. were inconclusive, a crevasse-fall seems likely. Any unroped and/or solo travel on Robson's—or any—glaciated terrain is ill-advised. (Source: Parks Canada Warden Service, Jim Mamalis)

FALL ON ROCK, FAILURE TO FOLLOW ROUTE, PROTECTION PULLED OUT
British Columbia, Bugaboo Glacier Provincial Park/Alpine Recreation Area, Snowpatch Spire

On August 2, having climbed through the squeeze chimney, two climbers were ascending the final pitch of the Kraus/McCarthy route on Snowpatch Spire. The lead climber mistakenly assumed the 5.10 crack under the anchor was the 5.8 crack in the Kraus/McCarthy route description. After moving through a layback, he selected to reach for the anchor rather than reverse down the layback. The crack is fist-sized towards the top. Cams of the correct size had been used up lower down on the pitch. The lead climber fell just below the summit ridge. The top-most nut and cam ripped from the crack and the climber hit the ledge below, landing on his back. Shortly thereafter, two other climbers were descending the Kraus/McCarthy and were able to help with the rappels.

Analysis

The old topo from the first edition of Randall and Greene's guidebook for the area indicates a bolted anchor above the 5.8 crack. The new edition correctly shows the anchor well to the right of the crack (above the 5.10b crack). The ledge below would have provided a good belay station that could have been used to bring up the second and re-rack gear. Better analysis of the route, as well as possibly splitting the pitch into two pitches to allow gear to be reused, might have changed the results. (Source: Stephane Durocher)

FALL ON ROCK
British Columbia, Squamish, Lower Malamute area

On August 6, a 23-year-old male from the United States fell while rock climbing in an area known as the Lower Malamute. He narrowly missed hitting the railroad tracks when he fell. He was transported to the Squamish Hospital assisted by employees of BC Rail with possible back injuries.

Analysis

This is the second incident of this type in the last few weeks where a climber has fallen in the same area. The RCMP and BC Rail would like to remind the public that this area is on BC Rail property and it is illegal and unsafe to be in this area climbing or for any other reason. Signs identifying that this is Private Property have now been placed in the area. (Source: RCMP, BC Media)

FALL INTO CREVASSE, PLACED INADEQUATE PROTECTION, TIME OF DAY
British Columbia, Mount Robson Provincial Park, Mount Robson

On August 31, Richard Denker (48) and Bob Breivogel (52) were making their way up the Robson Glacier to the Dome. At 1645 while weaving through the "Mousetrap," a crevasse field at approximately 2,900 meters, Breivogel fell through a snow bridge over a crevasse. Blocks of snow which had bridged the crevasse fell onto the climber while he hung upside down from the rope, six meters below the lip. The falling debris caused rib and shoulder injuries. A second group of two climbers in the area assisted Denker in getting his partner out of the crevasse and back down the glacier to 2,700 meters where they spent the night.

The assisting climbers left for help at 1900 reaching the Berg Lake Ranger Station at 0130 on September 1. A Parks Canada rescue team was contacted and the two climbers were evacuated using a helicopter and sling rescue system. Upon arrival at the hospital, it was determined that Breivogel had broken ribs and was suffering from a pneumothorax. (Source: Parks Canada Warden Service, Jim Mamalis)

Analysis

A couple of things come to mind. One, we were still crossing the ice-fall late in the day and late in the season. An earlier start or a higher camp may have helped. Second, we were using a doubled 70-meter (9mm) rope and were tied to the very ends, so a "tighter" belay and/or picket protection placed where the route made bends may have helped in reducing the length of the fall. However, the latter may not have helped in preventing the injuries, because they were the result of snow and ice blocks falling on Bob, not from the fall itself or the length of the fall. Also, when Bob righted himself in the crevasse, he was only about 12 to 18 feet below the lip. The rope stretch over the 35 meters of rope between us would be enough to cause the fall to be this distance.

In the dangerous area of the icefall, it would have been better either to be closer together or to belay the leader at bridges on a relatively short lead rope. Also, icefall crevasses—actually gaps in the icefall rubble—are unlike crevasses in snow-covered glaciers. Icefall crevasse bridges are made of smaller ice rubble which can seem sold when probing, but can break unexpectedly. The ice chunks are obviously more dangerous than soft snow when they fall on the victim.

We were probably over confident due to our extensive glacier experience on the volcanoes in the Northwest. These are usually climbed early to mid-season. We were lucky to have another party nearby to aid in the rescue, to have favorable weather and a good emergency camp location, and to experience an efficient rescue by the Canadian authorities. (Source: Paraphrased from a report submitted by Richard Denkler)

FALL ON ICE, INADEQUATE PROTECTION, PROTECTION (TOOLS) PULLED OUT

New Brunswick, The Quarry

Description: On March 1, three experienced climbers set out for a day of ice climbing at a climbing area known as the Quarry in New Brunswick. G.P., the leader for the first climb selected a moderate 25-meter single-pitch climb that he had led before. The ice appeared to be continuous on the climb and good although not fat. The first two-thirds of the single-pitch climb went smoothly with three or four seemingly solid placements leading up to a short vertical section. The last placement was a pound-in screw at the level of the bottom of the vertical section but slightly off to the right. Placement of protection on the vertical section was considered but ruled out due to the vertical section being short and the ice on the vertical section not being as solid as it had appeared from below. As the lead moved onto the vertical section, it became apparent that there was better ice and an easier stance slightly to the left of center on the vertical section. The top of the vertical was reached with a couple of moves. The vertical section ended in an ice-covered ledge approximately 15 meters above the start of the climb. The move onto the ledge appeared to be straightforward with a bulge on the right side above and back away from the edge. G.P. placed the right tool in this bulge and the left tool in blue horizontal ice that was also back from the edge. The higher risk of fracture of a bulge was considered but ignored in light of the sound and feel of the right hand tool placement, the perceived quality of the left placement, and the low level of difficulty of the move. As G.P. was pulling up to gain the ledge, the bulge on the right shattered and released the tool. G.P. vividly recalls thinking that the left arm was likely susceptible to some discomfort as a result of a drop-down onto that arm. G.P. also vividly recalls apprehension resulting from the sudden realization that the left tool was also coming free of the ice. He fell about three meters before striking a ramp with his left foot, breaking the left leg at the ankle, and then tumbling backwards. The runout from the highest protection was such that the rope provided no tension until after the leader struck the ramp with his foot. After tumbling backward, he slid headfirst on his back down a steep ramp until the tension of the rope stopped the slide. The length of the slide was longer than necessary. The lowest piece of protection was a pound-in screw that pulled out under the directional force and the belay stance was away from and off to one side of the base of the climb resulting in additional slack in the system. The leader was lowered from the climb and assisted onto a makeshift stretcher by his two climbing partners. The carry down a steep 50-meter slope and another 800 meters through deep snow to a road took 2.5 hours. The last half-hour was with assistance from two additional people. An alternate to the approach route was selected for the evacuation because it was more direct and less obstructed by brush.

Analysis

G.P. states he has learned some lessons:

Never trust a bulge.

Do not underestimate the horizontal forces exerted on tool placements while topping out.

As with rock climbing give due consideration to location, type, and placement of the first protection if the belayer is not immediately below that piece and subsequent protection.

Know your first aid and self-rescue techniques.

Consider possible means of evacuation of an injured climber before accidents occur.

The Canadian editor would add that the riskiest moves are pulling over a lip or a bulge where the angle of the ice changes. Wherever possible, the leader should place protection before attempting to move from vertical ground over a bulge or ledge. A leader should always be considering how far down his last piece is and the likelihood of hitting ledges on the way down.

In this respect moderate climbs can be more dangerous than truly vertical terrain if a fall occurs. Lower extremity fractures such as this are a common result. (Source: George Porter and Edwina Podemski)

(Editor's Note: Edwina Podemski did all the analyses where no name appears as a source.)

MEXICO

FALLING ROCK–DISLODGED ROCK
Monterrey, El Potrero Chico, Space Boyz

On December 29, my climbing partner, Crockett Farnell, and I (Gordon Wright) were climbing the 11-pitch route Space Boyz on the west side of El Potrero Chico, near Monterrey, Mexico. We had just completed the two hardest pitches (6 and 7). I was belaying at the bottom of the eighth pitch and Crockett had just arrived at the anchors above me. A Mexican father - and-son team of climbers had been following us up the route throughout the day. The son, in his mid-to-late twenties, was about two-thirds of the way up the seventh pitch, just below and to the right of me. He suddenly shouted a desperate warning in Spanish. I looked down and saw that he had knocked loose a large rock, at least one cubic foot (one-third a cubic meter) in size. I watched in horror as it fell directly toward the red-helmeted head of his father, who was belaying from a narrow ledge below. The man managed to dodge slightly into the corner and, with great relief, I saw that the rock narrowly missed his helmet. However, it crashed onto the ledge, broke into a number of large pieces and began raining down over the faces and slabs below. Both the son and I kept shouting, "Rock over Space Boyz!" in both Spanish and English, as the pieces bounced, broke, and ricocheted their way down the mountain. There were many climbers at different heights on various routes below and I was terribly afraid that the falling debris could injure numerous people. There was bedlam for a long, frightening moment.

Finally, the rock fall subsided and people stopped shouting. An eerie silence filled the canyon as everyone waited to learn who was hurt. Thankfully and mi-raculously, there were no immediate cries of pain or distress. Just as I shook my head in relief, however, a long, pitiful wail was broadcast out across the canyon. It came from the red-helmeted man on the ledge below me. The son anxiously called down to his father and received more cries of pain in response. He busily tied himself off to a bolted hanger, then looked up at me with frightened eyes and pleaded, "Please, my father, please help me!" As my stomach turned over and adrenaline hit my bloodstream, I answered, "Yes, we will come down." And, although I meant it, I was suddenly afraid of what we might find down there and, being untrained in rescue procedures, afraid that we wouldn't know what to do once we got there.

I called up to Crockett, told him the man below was hurt, and said we needed to go down to help. After lowering Crockett from the chains above, both of us rappelled down to the son and his father on the narrow, exposed ledge where the accident had occurred. Fortunately, there are numerous bolted anchors there and we were all able to adequately secure ourselves. I estimate we were 700 feet (212 meters) above the ground. The son, whose name, we learned, is Oscar, spoke a little English, and Crockett speaks a little Spanish. We determined that the rock had struck the father (later identified as Zenon

Rosas Franco, 49) on his right leg and broken the femur. It was a closed fracture, but he was in tremendous pain. One of his hands also appeared to be injured. When Zenon began shouting in anguish, Oscar—who was terribly upset but resolutely in control of himself—reprimanded his father in Spanish, telling him to be strong and not to yell. There was nothing to splint the leg with, so Oscar used a sling to wrap and support his father's thigh. He then had the good sense to check their single 60-meter rope for damage and found that the rock had punctured the core near the rope's mid-point. He knotted off the damaged section. I was impressed by Oscar's courage and presence of mind.

Crockett and I had two 60-meter ropes with us. While we sorted the loops and piles of nylon around us, we slowly worked out a plan for lowering the injured Zenon. I rappelled to the station below and, using a cordelette, built a sturdy anchor that would provide multiple tie-in points. Oscar and Crockett then lowered Zenon to me on a second rope. The first two lowers were tricky because the stations were not vertically aligned. We clipped Zenon to my rappel line with a quickdraw, so I was able to pull him laterally across the face (and, in the first instance, around a corner) while he was being lowered. I then did my best to anchor him in a position that offered his leg some stability. Oscar joined us next in order to remain close to his father, leaving Crockett to clean the previous anchor, rappel down, and pull the ropes.

Word of the accident had been communicated to the Mexican authorities and, after some time, police and emergency vehicles began arriving below. Many climbers lowered off their routes and gathered at the base of Space Boyz, seeking ways to lend assistance. Others, however, continued climbing their routes uninterrupted. After the two difficult lowers, we arrived at a sizable ledge where we recouped for a few minutes. It was then that a huge rescue helicopter from Monterrey arrived. It came whomping into the canyon and hovered near us. Not wishing to complicate matters further and feeling confident we could successfully lower Zenon down the remaining four pitches, we waved the helicopter off. The pilot found a landing site at the south end of the canyon.

Two other climbers then arrived at our ledge, one of them bearing a leg splint borrowed from an emergency vehicle. They told us they had fixed a single rope to the ground from the top of the second pitch below us. As I rappelled the fourth pitch and built another anchor, the others splinted Zenon's leg and moved him into position for the next lower. The splint appeared to ease his suffering considerably, but he remained in much pain. His hand seemed to be bothering him at that time as well.

From the beginning of our inexpert rescue effort, we had remained concerned about the confusion created by the number of people, number of ropes, and many slings and carabiners present at each set of anchors. We were very careful to ensure that everyone and everything was properly secured at all times. While on the large ledge, however, Crockett caught the arm of one of the recently-arrived climbers just as the fellow was about to back off the ledge. Apparently, he was about to lower off on a single rope he assumed was fixed but was, in fact, set up for rappel. Thanks to Crockett's attention and quick action, a second accident may have been averted. Zenon was lowered to me at the top of pitch three, during which several strategically placed cactus plants added insult to his injury. Oscar then joined us, as was our established procedure. It was then that our day was brightened by the arrival of Patrick Delaney at the anchors immediately below. As it turned out, Patrick is a certified Canadian mountain guide and rescue specialist from Squamish, British Columbia. When the accident first occurred, he and his girlfriend were seven pitches up on a route across the canyon. They immediately began a two-hour descent in order to come to our assistance. (At one point, Patrick said, there were seven people lined up at a set of anchors waiting to go up or down!) After consulting with the emergency response people on the ground, Patrick ascended the fixed rope to the top of the second pitch. From there he called up and asked various questions about Zenon's injuries and condition. He relayed this information to those on the ground.

Oscar and I then lowered Zenon to Patrick, who was pre-rigged to rappel with Zenon to the ambulance waiting below. Within several minutes, the injured climber was safely in the care of the Mexican emergency people.

I told Oscar to go down next in order to accompany his father to the hospital. By then, quite understandably, he was beginning to unravel emotionally and I encouraged him to remain careful throughout the remainder of his descent. He thoughtfully expressed his thanks and gratitude to Crockett and me before he safely rappelled the remaining three pitches to the ground. I went down next and then Crockett joined me after rappelling four pitches from the ledge. We pulled the last of the ropes, packed our gear, and went off in search of cold beer. (The other two climbers had continued up the route after helping with the splint.) In all, the rescue took just over four hours to complete. I credit both Oscar and Zenon for their courage and strength and wish them well.

Analysis

El Potrero Chico has a reputation for rock fall. (Such was the cause of the most recent fatality there.) Crockett and I were aware of this hazard upon our arrival at the Potrero and, to the best of our ability, were cautious when climbing and rappelling. We were also reluctant to climb in exposed areas beneath other parties. Despite these efforts, however, Crockett narrowly missed getting whacked by a rock the size of my fist that I managed to knock loose several days after the accident.

Just ten or fifteen minutes before the accident on Space Boyz, Crockett and I had both climbed the same pitch from which Oscar unloaded the rock on his father. I do not remember noticing a piece that large that looked dangerous, although I did notice many other potential bombs all over the Potrero. It may well be that Oscar had been in complete control and that the rock-fall was just pure, unavoidable misfortune. Or, he may have been climbing with some desperation, as the pitch is not a particularly easy one, and made a mistake. I cannot say which was the case; however, I can say that the damage potential from such a large piece being turned loose from that height was tremendous. Given the number of people climbing on that side of the canyon, it is remarkable that others were not injured that day. Constant evaluation of rock quality, careful testing for hollowness and looseness, judicious selection of foot and hand holds, and caution when hauling and tossing ropes could all help minimize the risk of similar accidents. Another important suggestion might be to use good judgment in route selection. The Potrero can become a very busy place, with line-ups below the area classics. There are sometimes four or more parties on the same route at various stages of ascent. This may not bode well for the late starters!

The lowering system we worked out proved relatively safe and successful, since the victim was conscious and able to participate to some degree in his rescue. On the two pitches that required lateral movement to reach the next anchors, it was particularly useful for me to go down first and "reel in" the victim on the extra rope while Oscar and Crockett lowered him. (The extra rope on long routes is, obviously, a good idea.) We were also fortunate that there are numerous bolted hangers at most stations on Space Boyz, which provided "bomber" security for the four of us.

Patrick Delaney later told us that, although the local emergency people had lots of equipment at their disposal, including hundreds of meters of static rope, he wasn't convinced that any of them knew what to do with it. He also felt the helicopter was too large to effect a safe evacuation from the air. Patrick was of the opinion that the victim would have spent the night up on the wall if we had not been in place to facilitate the rescue. I'm not sure how well Zenon would have dealt with that. The organization and training of a local rescue team (there are many capable climbers in Nuevo Leon) would be a great asset, since there are bound to be future accidents at the Potrero.

If the victim had been rendered unconscious, or had sustained more life-threatening injuries (such as a punctured artery in his broken leg), we'd have been in a serious pickle up there. Given the actual circumstances, I think we got off lucky. Knowledge and training are the obvious tools for dealing effectively with what might have been. More now than ever, I'm convinced that climbers should consider rescue techniques as important as pulling for that next grade of difficulty. We learned that a wonderful day at the crag can turn in your worst nightmare in an instant! And a final no-brainer: wear a helmet. (Source: Gordon Wright)

(Editor's Note: We are pleased to have a thorough report from Mexico. There are many "hear-say" reports that get conveyed, usually as a result of accidents on one of the volcanoes.)

UNITED STATES

RAPPEL FAILURE-INADEQUATE ANCHOR
Alaska, Moose's Tooth, Shaken Not Stirred

In the early morning of May 1, around 0200, Kevin Cooper and Ryan Jennings (ages unknown, as they did not register) were descending from the "Shaken Not Stirred" route on the Moose's Tooth. The two had begun their second-to-last rappel utilizing a slung block. Jennings was in the process of rappelling while Cooper waited at the anchor clipped off to the sling. The block began to pull away from the surrounding rock and fell. The two estimated their fall at approximately 1000 feet over both vertical terrain and angled snow slope. There were four other climbers in the area who heard the fall and responded to offer assistance.

Two climbing teams, Mark Westman and Joe Puryear and Seth Hobby and Coley Gentzel, assisted Cooper and Jennings to the rescuers' tent and stomped out SOS in the snow. Later that morning at 1115, a plane in the area operated by K2 aviation saw the distress signal and reported it to Talkeetna Air Taxi since they were known to have climbers in the area. By 1155, TAT reported to NPS that Roderick had picked up Cooper and Jennings and was en route back to Talkeetna.

Jennings had sustained a possible right tibia and fibula fracture while Cooper had an injury to his left knee.

Analysis

This incident is another reminder of the real hazards presented by rappelling and the difficulty of determining anchor security particularly in alpine environments where climbers are often relying on "natural" protection for part or all of their anchor system. Rock quality varies drastically throughout the Alaska Range, thus creating a particular need to carefully check all anchor systems. Another factor may have been above average temperatures causing a freeze-thaw cycle which loosened the block from its position. (Source: Ranger Margaret Perdue)

HAPE-ASCENDED TOO FAST
Alaska, Mount McKinley, West Buttress

On May 4, an Austrian party called Team Outback departed Talkeetna, for a climb of the West Buttress of Mount McKinley. Three days later the group arrived at the 14,200-foot camp. After one night there, the team attempted a carry to the 17,200-foot camp. After waking up on the morning of May 9 with a headache and ataxia, Karl Wieser (35) decided to seek NPS medical attention. Upon examination by NPS medical personnel, the climber presented with crackles in both the right and left lung as well as significant dyspnea on exertion. It was determined that he was suffering from HAPE.

Treatment consisted of Nifedipine, Diamox, and oxygen therapy. Due to weather conditions it was determined that decent was not appropriate. After four day's of monitoring and treatment, weather conditions improved and the climber was released from NPS medical care and placed on low-flow oxygen for descent to the 7,200-foot camp with his teammates.

Analysis

Although altitude illness such as HAPE can still occur to climbers who take an appropriate amount of time to acclimatize, it is much more probable and common to happen to climbers who rush their ascent. Team Outback was an experienced climbing party that had been to higher altitudes. However, their three-day ascent to the 14,200-foot camp was faster than the recommended minimum of five days that parties should spend acclimatizing on their ascent to that camp. The quick ascent along with the fact that the team then decided to attempt to go directly to the 17,200-foot camp without taking any rest days no doubt exacerbated any potential altitude illness. (Source: Ranger John Leonard)

FROSTBITE, AMS
Alaska, Mount McKinley, West Buttress

In the early morning of May 14, the team New River George contacted NPS personnel stationed at the 14,200-foot camp and alerted them about a climbing party called Team Homer Company. The former had been monitoring Homer's descent and believed they were calling for help. NPS personnel monitored the situation and determined that the climbers were indeed calling for help. After making NPS personnel in Talkeetna aware of the situation, rangers at the 14,200-foot camp mobilized available resources and devised a strategy to respond to Team Homer Company's location.

Around 0300 a team consisting of NPS patrol members and emergency hired independent climbers left for their suspected location. Shortly there after as daylight allowed they were spotted by rangers and subsequently met by the ground team that had departed the 14,200-foot camp.

After being accompanied back, the climbers were evaluated by NPS medical personnel and it was determined that one of the two, Steve Normandin (29) was suffering from frostbite to both hands, both feet, and his nose. He also had signs and symptoms of Acute Mountain Sickness (AMS). He was admitted for additional medical care and observation at 0500.

NPS patrol member Keith Thompson, MD, began treatment that included rapid rewarming of the patient's hands and feet as well as the use of Toradol for pain relief. after rewarming the extremities where appropriately medicated and dressed. On the afternoon of May 14, the patient was released from NPS medical care and began the descent to the 7,200-foot camp for transport to Talkeetna.

Analysis

Though Team Homer Company would later claim not to have been calling for help, it appeared to those present at the 14,200-foot camp that not only were they calling for help, they were making desperate pleas for assistance. Decisions to put personnel in the field to assist with a potential rescue are not ones that are made in haste or taken lightly. Everything that was presented to NPS personnel at the time led them to believe that indeed

Team Homer Company was in a dire situation. In the end, they did end up requiring NPS assistance whether or not they had originally called for it. (Source: Ranger John Leonard)

ILLNESS–COLITIS
Alaska, Mount McKinley, West Buttress

At 1825 on May 19, Christopher Allewell (age unknown) was assisted into the 14,200-foot NPS medical tent by his teammates. His chief complaint was severe abdominal pain and a mild headache. Upon examination, pain was localized in his mid quadrant, bilaterally, with a severity of ten on a scale of one to ten, ten being the most painful. Pain was not associated with vomiting or fever. However, Allewell expressed extreme tenderness and guarding of his abdomen. Symptoms occurred suddenly and had been apparent for approximately six prior to his arrival at the NPS medical tent. Past medical history did not indicate a cause. Bowel sounds were present and urination was clear. Allewell's pain was mildly relieved when he lay in a left lateral recumbent position. After conferring with Dr. Jennifer Dow, NPS volunteer Steve Stein started an IV. Two liters of intravenous fluids were given. No pain medications were administered at this time.

By the morning of May 20, Allewell's pain had increased in his upper right quadrant and had radiated into his back. Though his headache was relieved, Allewell's abdominal pain persisted, dramatically affecting his mobility. At 1257, Dr. Jennifer Dow authorized 30mg of Toradol for pain relief and recommended an immediate evacuation. At 1500, Allewell was transported to the 7,200-foot basecamp by the NPS contract helicopter and then flown to Regional Hospital in Anchorage by the LifeGuard helicopter.

Analysis

In the hospital, Allewell was diagnosed with colitis, an inflammation of the gut wall. Colitis requires surgery only when infectious. Lack of oxygen (i.e. altitude) can cause an infection, and therefore Allewell remained under observation in the hospital for several days.

Unfortunately, Allewell could not have predicted or prevented his condition or need for evacuation. However, Allewell's situation did reflect the difficulty of treating abdominal pain while in the backcountry. Determining the source of the pain can be extremely difficult. In Allewell's case, duration and severity indicated the need to evacuate. Extreme tenderness, guarding, the inability to move, and pain threshold were the key elements used to assess the severity of his condition. As a rescuer, patient assessment is a critical skill in order to determine acute abdominal pain and the need for immediate evacuation. (Source: Ranger Karen Hilton)

DEHYDRATION, UNABLE TO GET TO MITTENS–FROSTBITE
Alaska, Mount McKinley, West Rib

On May 3rd, the three-member expedition, Rocky Mountain West Rib, led by Fabrizio Zangrilli, flew in to the Kahiltna Glacier to attempt the West

Rib. On the 17th, they ascended the 1200-foot West Rib Couloir. On this ascent, Roger Pennington (age unknown), a member of the expedition, frostbit several of his fingers. Pennington felt both dehydration and the inability to get to his heavy mittens when he needed them caused the frostbite. They spent that night on a small ice ledge at the top of the couloir. The next day they moved up to the Apex Camp at 12,900 feet. Over the course of these two days, Pennington felt he had thawed, refrozen and thawed his left ring finger.

On the 20th they moved to a 13,300-foot camp where as a group they decided that Pennington needed to be evacuated because of his frostbite and slow pace. At 0956, Zangrilli requested assistance through his aircraft radio to a scenic flight overhead, flown by Eric Denkewalter of Talkeetna Aero Services. At 1012, Zangrilli described frostbite on two fingers of Pennington's right hand and the ring finger on his left. Ranger Daryl Miller stated that the helicopter was not available on that day and recommended that the expedition continue to the 14,800-foot bergschrund camp where they would be in a safe place if weather changed. A call-back time was set at 1800. The NPS chartered Talkeetna Air Taxi to fly Ranger Roger Robinson for this call-back. While on this flight at 1805, Zangrilli indicated that they had only made it to the 14,500-foot level and were digging in. Zangrilli still insisted on the rescue, and he was informed that the Park Service would try the next morning.

On May 21st at 1000, the contract Lama helicopter with pilot Jim Hood and manager Dave Kreutzer departed Talkeetna en route to the West Rib. The Lama was on scene at 1046 where it was determined that a shorthaul using the basket could be accomplished. The Lama proceeded to the 14,200-foot camp where the shorthaul was rigged and then returned at 1052 extracting Pennington in the basket. Pennington was first shorthauled to the 14,200-foot camp and then transported inside the Lama to Kahiltna Basecamp, then to Talkeetna. Once in Anchorage, Pennington was diagnosed with superficial to partial thickness frostbite on the first digit of three of his fingers.

Analysis

Pennington's frostbite is very typical of what is seen frequently by the rangers at 14,200 feet. The Ranger Staff felt that Pennington would not need a rescue and could probably descend via the West Buttress if he could only get there. The big question was whether Pennington could ascend to 15,200 feet on the West Rib, because then he could easily reach the 14,200-foot camp.

Once the Rocky Mountain West Rib party had made up their mind that Pennington was not going higher, then we were left with two options —either doing a ground rescue or an air evacuation. Since slope conditions were unknown between 14,500 feet and 15,200 feet, it was felt that the least risk to personnel was to use the Lama helicopter. If Pennington had been climbing on the West Buttress he would have been told to walk down. (Source: Ranger Roger Robinson)

ANKLE INJURY AND HAPE
Alaska, Mount McKinley, West Buttress

This summary is comprised of two separate incidents that ended up as one continuous effort using many shared resources and with multiple overlapping responsibilities.

On May 26 Lee Jung Park (age unknown) of the "Duksung Women's University Alpine Team Expedition" injured her ankle when her leg "gave out" while descending the West Buttress route on Mt. McKinley around 16,500 feet, just below "Washburn's Thumb." Park was lowered by her teammates with assistance from another Korean team that was descending from the 17,200-foot camp at the same time. On May 28, Park was evacuated from 14,200-foot camp to the 7,200-foot base camp by the National Park Service (NPS) contract Lama helicopter.

On May 27, Todd Passey (age unknown), a guide for Alpine Ascents International, was diagnosed with High Altitude Pulmonary Edema. Passey was put on oxygen, given Nifedpine and remained under observation overnight. On May 28, Passey, (along with Park) was evacuated by the NPS contract Lama helicopter to the 7,200-foot camp where he was transferred to a fixed-wing aircraft and transported to Talkeetna.

Analysis

The "Duksung Women's University Alpine Team Expedition," with help from another party, were able to execute a self-rescue and lowering of the patient in an efficient manner to within 100-200 meters of the 14,200-foot camp without the help of NPS personnel. Though the NPS took over care of the patient very close to camp, this self-initiated rescue effort, in poor weather conditions, is the type of behavior that is necessary in this environment to achieve a favorable outcome for the injured party. Had this team waited for the Park Service to respond, it would have taken a much longer time to get resources into place and may have resulted in cold related injuries much worse than those that were sustained during the lowering.

As for the HAPE case, everyone has the potential to be afflicted—even guides. Early recognition and descent are the keys to survival. Oxygen therapy will buy the patient time, but the best and most effective treatment is always to descend to a lower elevation. The patient's team was initially planning on descending on the morning of the 28th, but with the Lama coming in to evacuate Park, it was determined that fewer people would be put at risk if Passey were evacuated. The decision to evacuate an injured climber via helicopter always requires a thorough risk assessment and is a decision that the Park Service Rangers never take lightly. (Source: Ranger Gordy Kito)

STRAINED BACK
Alaska, Mount McKinley, West Buttress

On the afternoon of June 2, an RMI guided group was ascending below the fixed lines around 15,000 feet when assistant guide Ryan Sorsdahl (24) twisted awkwardly and felt something "pop" in his lower back. Keil Hillman, lead guide, assessed him and concluded that he could not continue up. He contacted the 14,200-foot Ranger Camp and informed Ranger Evans of this via CB radio. As Sorsdahl could move under his own power without a load on his back, it was decided to send up VIP Dave Hanning to assist Sorsdahl down. As the location was considered to be in a safe area, Hanning ascended by himself, then carried Sorsdahl's backpack down while escorting him.

At the Ranger Camp Sorsdahl was examined by Medic Michael Dong, who diagnosed the damage to the soft tissue of the sacroiliac area involving the sciatic nerve. As a result, it was decided that Sorsdahl should ideally not walk down as further damage might occur. However, there was no urgency for evacuation. On June 4th the NPS contracted Lama helicopter was performing another rescue and took Sorsdahl from the Ranger Camp down to Base Camp where he flew out by fixed wing prior to medical examination.

Analysis

This was an unfortunate accident that, luckily for the group, occurred at a location where assistance was readily available. There is no doubt that if this had been in a more remote location the group would have had to give up on their climb and bring Sorsdahl down themselves. As it was we were able to easily give assistance and to include the med-evac in conjunction with another flight into the mountain. Medically this was also the best for Sorsdahl. (Source: Ranger John Evans)

FALL ON SNOW–INADEQUATE PROTECTION, HASTE
Alaska, Mount McKinley, West Buttress

This incident happened in May while we were descending the fixed lines of the West Buttress. We happened to be the only roped team (as well as our other two climbing partners ahead of us on another roped team) allowing for the team ahead of us to get off the fixed line before we got on it, but many people were right on our tails on the way down. My partner and I were spaced out exactly one fixed rope length apart, so that when I reached the anchor to switch over to the next fixed line down, my partner would be getting onto the fixed line I was on previously. Just as he did this and just switched over from his fixed line (second to the last), a climber only five feet behind him slipped and fell. The climber hit the anchor but had a runner over five feet long, so he fell five feet below the anchor, jabbing my partner in the leg with his crampon. My partner went into ice ax arrest, but on the steep blue ice with a full pack, he couldn't hold it for long and so he fell the full fixed line length before hitting the anchor below (just a few feet above me). As the anchor caught him, he swung around and his pack hit me in the shoulder and knocked me off. I didn't fall nearly as far, as my crampon caught in the remaining line not anchored, as it was the last line getting off the fixed lines and not secured with a picket. However, I was upside down with my back laying against the snow and my ax had pinned me in such a way that if I sat up, it crammed down on my arm. So my partner had to come down using his Tibloc so I could right myself. I consider myself in excellent shape, at 5'8" and 155 pounds. I climb sport and trad at a high level. But I felt so helpless in this predicament, even though I was on a fairly low angle (maybe 45 degrees at this point) slope. I came out of it with no injuries, but my buddy was less fortunate. He had the puncture wound from the crampon in his thigh and had tweaked his knee, but was able to descend under his own power, albeit slowly, and he was in pain. The climber who hit him caught up to us and apologized emphatically.

Upon reaching 14,200 feet, we had Ranger John Evans assess my partner and determined that with deteriorating weather coming in, the helicopter would not be able to pull him off for a few days. He decided to make a go of it down, but knew that once he started he would not be able to stop due to swelling and pain. We unloaded all of his gear and divided it up between two roped teams. We used skis as our mode of transportation on the lower slopes, but my partner was not able to put skis on until the more mellow five-mile "traverse" from 7,900 feet to basecamp. We made it out in one push.

Analysis
Often teams want to get down the mountain in a hurry, to get back to the 14,200-foot camp and not wait until the team ahead of them is off the first fixed line. Coupled with no breaking devices on the fixed lines, just using an arm rap with two cordelettes with 'biners to act as runners on the fixed lines, it means that when one climber falls, he takes out the others below him. (Source: Ryland Moore)

KNEE INJURY, INEXPERIENCE
Alaska, Mount McKinley, West Buttress
On May 30, the two members of the Sled Dog expedition, Matt Sachs (34) and June Braugham (40) were evacuated from the 14,200-foot camp on Denali. On the 29th, Sachs sustained a knee injury while climbing to the fixed lines and requested ranger assistance to descend. Sachs was lowered approximately 1,200 feet by NPS personnel to the 14,200-foot Ranger Camp where he received medical assistance for the night. Sachs was flown to 7,000-foot camp the following morning by the Denali Lama helicopter. Due to her very limited mountain experience, Braugham accompanied Sachs to Denali basecamp after it was deemed unsafe for her to continue climbing on the mountain.

Analysis
It is likely Sachs' prior knee injury contributed to its final blow-out. By avoiding consecutive days of heavy use on a weakened knee, Sachs could have better monitored the extent of his previous injury. Once evaluated by a doctor, it was determined that Sachs damaged his lateral and medial collateral ligaments. With no additional damage to surrounding ligaments, injury may have resulted from the cumulative use of a sprained knee. Having a CB radio did prove beneficial in expediting a rescue. However, choosing

a climbing partner ill-suited for Denali created a compromising situation for the climbing rangers, the National Park Service, June Braugham, and Matt Sachs himself in deciding the safest means of descent for Braugham. (Source: Ranger Karen Hilton)

HAPE
Alaska, Mount McKinley, West Buttress

On June 1, Peter Staples (48) of the "OSAT,03" expedition, suffered from High Altitude Pulmonary Edema (HAPE) while camping at the 17,200-foot camp on Mt. McKinley's West Buttress route. Staples was assisted by his team and National Park Service (NPS) Ranger Gordy Kito and NPS Volunteer In Park (VIP) Ryan Davis from the 17,200-foot camp to the 14,200-foot Ranger camp, where he was monitored and released. Staples was able to continue with his team down to the 7,200-foot Kahiltna base camp under his own power and without further incident.

Analysis

The amount of time that the "OSAT,03" expedition took to get to high camp was within the timeframe recommended by the NPS. Mr. Staples may have been able to increase his chances of acclimatizing well by taking even more time getting to the 17,200-foot camp. However, this technique may or may not have reduced the likelihood of his being stricken with HAPE. Like most cases of HAPE, Mr. Staples presented with only very mild symptoms of Acute Mountain Sickness (AMS) the first night at the 17,200-foot camp. Only after spending two nights at 17,200 feet did Mr. Staples present with audible rales and a debilitating shortness of breath. The quick actions of Mr. Staples and his team members in recognizing his condition as life threatening and rapid notification of the NPS staff, as well as the fortuitous placement of the Rangers contributed to the positive outcome of this incident.

It is worth noting that Mr. Staples fellow team members contacted the NPS Rangers with the intention of locating oxygen and descending with their ill teammate without assistance from NPS personnel. This self suffi-cient and responsible behavior that some teams display on Mount McKinley may be the result of the information and education program initiated by the NPS some years ago. This program focuses on informing climbers about the risks associated with high altitude mountaineering and the things they can do to help reduce their exposure to some of those risks and the possible result of these inherent dangers, up to and including death. (Source: Ranger Gordy Kito)

DEHYDRATION–EXHAUSTION, MINOR FROSTBITE, CLIMBING TOO SLOWLY–FAILURE TO TURN BACK
Alaska, Mount McKinley, Messner Couloir

At 0500 on June 3, Jan Markup (27), Petr Hoffman (27) from the Czech Republic, and Camelo Lopez from a Colombian-American expedition, who had asked to climb with the Czechs, left the 14,200-foot camp to attempt the Messner Couloir from which the Czech "Cheechakos" had been turned back by poor snow conditions a few days earlier. They moved very slowly all day and reached the top of the steep part of the couloir approximately 2200. They still had a rocky exit to negotiate but at an easier angle than the main couloir.

On June 4, Natalie Lopez from the Colombian-American team came to the 14,200 foot camp and stated that the party in the Messner Couloir was in difficulties. She was in contact with the party via a talkabout radio. When Ranger Evans contacted Camelo Lopez, he stated that he had frostbitten his feet and was hypothermic but that the other two were ok. At 0256, Evans asked Lopez if they could make it over the top of the Couloir to the Normal West Buttress Route to descend, as no rescue would be able to reach them for at least eight hours. Lopez agreed to try and it was arranged for them to check in every 30 minutes.

At 0338, Jan and Petr stated that Lopez could not move and was not coherent, and that they could not get him any higher up the couloir. They said they would try to get food and water into Lopez and hold their position. At 0414, Jan and Petr stated that Lopez had stopped talking, he has very cold, probably frostbitten, feet, and was in a bad way. They were still trying to get food and water in to him.

At 0426 South District Ranger in Talkeetna was informed of situation. At 0444, Lopez sounded moderately sensible on the radio, stated that his feet were frozen (white and waxy), and that one of the others had frostbite on his hands. They cannot move from their location due to the steepness and their condition.

At 0523, Jan reports that Lopez was deteriorating again. They are still drinking warm liquids but Lopez has vomited. At 0540 Lopez reports that they were having trouble maintaining. An overhead team was assembled in Talkeetna at 0545, and a briefing on the situation given to them.

At 0609, Lopez stated that his legs would not work, and at 0630, Lopez stated that he did not think that they can last more than an hour. They are told to stay focused and to make sure harnesses etc. are on correctly. Asked if Jan and Petr can walk down safely if Lopez is evacuated, they reply that they do not think that they can make it down safely, as they are now cold and exhausted.

At 0700, plans were discussed with Talkeetna for a possible helicopter evacuation. At 0752, rangers at the 14,200 foot camp were still trying to persuade Lopez and Hoffman and Markup to walk. Lopez says pain is still too much to walk and Hoffman and Markup are to exhausted to walk down safely.

At 0936, the Lama takes off from Talkeetna and at 1020 does a reconnaissance flight over the evacuation site and the crew decided to use the rescue basket. At 1051 the Lama picks up Lopez and returns him to Base Camp, then returns twice to pick up Jan and Petr and fly them to Base Camp by 1150.

Patient assessments after arrival at Base Camp: Camelo Lopez—minor frostbite to toes, possible AMS, dehydrated, hypothermic and exhausted. Jan Markup—exhaustion, dehydrated. Petr Hoffman—exhaustion, dehydrated.

Analysis

This incident was the result of a lot of small mistakes compounding themselves and creating a major problem. Mistakes included adding an extra person to the team at short notice, especially a person of unknown ability; the fact that three people do not move as quickly as two; the fact that each person had only two liters of water and did not stop to make more until problems started; and perhaps most significantly, climbing very slowly (17 hours from camp to the top of the difficulties) and not making a decision to turn around.

Although it is a good idea to have the means to contact other people, in this case "Talkabout" radios, one cannot help but wonder whether this also gives parties an easy way out; that is, to call for rescue sooner than really needed or to continue in the belief that with communication they have a safety net and therefore continue when they should consider turning around. If this party had not had the means to contact the Rangers, would they have been able to get themselves to safety or would things have been made worse? A question we will never be able to answer. However, the Rangers responded (as they should) on the strength of the information (sometimes suspect) received over the radio, asking the helicopter crew to perform a risky operation at an extremely high altitude (19,000 feet), but it could easily have been a ground team at risk executing a potentially hazardous rescue. It is incumbent on all climbers to assess the possibility of self-evacuation/rescue before requesting outside assistance, especially before they even start on a climb as committing and remote as the Messner Couloir.

As a footnote, it is worth noting that the Talkeetna Ranger Station is reviewing its rescue policies. At present it is expected that if a party is rescued, they will not just be allowed to continue climbing, but rather, be returned to Talkeetna for a thorough debrief. This is both to ascertain all the facts of the case and insure the physical well being of all parties concerned. (Source: Ranger John Evans)

DENTAL-LACERATION AND BICUSPID FRACTURE
Alaska, Mount McKinley, West Buttress

On June 5th, RMI guide Brent Okita brought a 17-year-old client to the 14,200-foot medical tent to have a dental check. The prior day, the client was eating a frozen nougat bar, and bent a braces collar outwards which presently was lacerating the inside of the client's cheek. The braces' wires had been removed by the client's orthodontist prior to the expedition, with the collars left in place for later removal. The cheek laceration was minor, although consistently in the same site and reopening with any mandible movement.

Then on June 6th, a climber presented with a fracture of the first bicuspid, maxillary right side. The dentin had been exposed and he was in discomfort when eating/drinking and breathing the cold air through the mouth. Cavit (temporary cement) was applied to the site with saliva as the material setting agent.

Analysis

The first case is an intriguing one, as this is not one a medic ever expects. Upon examination of the client, it was apparent the collar was bent in such a way that covering it with Cavit or wax would be of little benefit. Confirming the brace collars were to be removed in the near future, I utilized the tools available: a needle holder and a nut tool. Great care was necessary, as fracturing the enamel was a possibility. Careful manipulation eventually worked the collar into a loosened state, at which time it could be molded by the tools to curve over and off the molar. The client now has a souvenir from Denali. The cheek laceration would heal itself in time if kept rinsed and teeth brushed often. Oh, yes, don't forget to floss.

As for the second, if the fracture is completely through the tooth, or if the pulp is involved, this problem can result in a trip being ended. Cavit is a temporary material that can protect the dental tubules and smooth a fracture site. If Cavit is not available to cover a sharp edge, then a piece of emery cloth, a light file to the area, or sugarless gum will give temporary relief. In any case, an expedition would do well to keep some dental first-aid supplies in their kit. (Source: Michael W. Dong, VIP Mountaineering Ranger-Medic)

(Editor's Note: Thanks to Michael Dong for sending these forward, along with a few others. While not entered in the data as accidents, the situation is a good illustration of the need to be prepared for medical emergencies—or better yet as in this case, to avoid them by doing some preventive work.)

HACE
Alaska, Mount McKinley, West Buttress

At 1115 on June 13, Frank Brettholle (51), a member of the "Beer Run" expedition, was found unconscious by his team mates in his tent at the 17,200-foot high camp on Denali's West Buttress route. His team mates contacted Ranger Meg Perdue and volunteers who rendered medical aid and ground evacuated him to the 14,200-foot camp. After being monitored overnight there, Brettholle descended with his team to the 7,200-foot Kahiltna Base Camp on June 14. Once there, Brettholle again lapsed into unconsciousness. He was treated by Ranger Gordy Kito throughout the night and following day. Due to poor weather, Brettholle could not be evacuated until June 16, when he was taken by Air National Guard Pavehawk helicopter to Alaska Regional Hospital in Anchorage.

Analysis

This was a highly unusual case whose circumstances have not been closely paralleled by any previously known incidents on Denali. There was nothing to indicate, either in "Beer Run" expedition's acclimatization schedule or

Brettholle's physical state, his susceptibility to, nor the severity of the High Altitude Cerebral Edema he experienced. Even the previous incident of unconsciousness in the Cascades reported by his climbing partners was not necessarily pertinent to this situation, according to medical professionals. Nor did medical advisors feel there was any indication or significant risk of a relapse as was seen at base camp. For these reasons there seems little that could have been done differently to avoid this situation, though this experience will certainly now inform how subsequent cases are handled. In particular, it would be advisable to consider continuing treatment with Dexamethasone once initiated to guard against the possibility of relapse.

It is also worth noting and praising the level of commitment shown by this expedition in assisting their team mate and trying to remain as self-sufficient as possible while facing a difficult situation. They acted as a team, the significance of which should not be underestimated. (Source: Ranger Margaret Perdue)

INEXPERIENCE–PARTY SEPARATED AND UNROPED, DEHYDRATION–EXHAUSTION
Alaska, Mount McKinley, West Buttress

Just before 0600 on the morning of June 8, Alexey Volkov (27) contacted VIP Michael Dong at the 14,200-foot Ranger Camp. Volkov was concerned that one of his teammates, Sergiy Voytovych (28) had not yet arrived at camp. Dong awakened Ranger Meg Perdue to assist in determining the nature of the situation and the need for NPS involvement.

The team had started from the 11,200-foot camp the previous evening at 1900. Volkov and his other teammate, Eric Nazar (22), had last seen Voytovych just prior to Windy Corner (13,500 feet) about 0330. At that time Voytovych was 100 to 200 meters behind Volkov and Nazar and moving very slowly. Volkov and Nazar arrived at the 14,200-foot camp about 0500 and had decided to bivy in a campsite and await the arrival of Voytovych's, who was carrying the group's tent. Due to the snowy, windy conditions at that time, Volkov was concerned about Voytovych's condition, and was himself starting to become cold and unable to rest or sleep. When he contacted the rangers, Volkov expressed concern over the fact that the trail had been blowing over quickly and Voytovych was the least experienced member of the group with altitude experience only as high as 3000 meters. When asked how well the trail was wanded, Volkov stated they had placed wands. However, further questioning revealed they had only placed three wands out of the total of five they were carrying. At 0640 Nazar, the third member of the group, was brought to the Ranger Camp in an effort to gather more information and determine the ability of the team to assist their own team mate. During discussions with Volkov and Nazar, Volkov expressed his willingness to descend to look for Voytovych. However, it was pointed out to him that one of the possible scenarios for Voytovych's failure to arrive in camp was a crevasse fall, a real possibility in that area which is known for its crevasse hazard. Volkov responded that he would have no idea how to extricate his partner from such a situation.

Additionally, during this interview, Volkov was being treated for superficial and partial thickness frostbite he had sustained during the night. Nazar stated that because he had been out all night he did not feel capable of descending to look for his team mate.

Based on the information available and the stated inability of the team to provide assistance, Perdue contacted Talkeetna at 0710 to inform them of the situation and her intention to initiate a ground reconnaissance for Voytovych. Rob Gowler, a guide camped near the trail into the 14,200-foot camp, was asked to be on the lookout for Voytovych. Ranger Mik Shain and VIPs Tucker Chenoweth and Hans Hjelde were tasked with preparing to go out in search of Voytovych. At 0750 Gowler contacted Shain and informed him that Voytovych appeared to be coming up the hill into camp. Shain contacted the individual, who did turn out to be Voytovych, and determined that he was fine, though exhausted and dehydrated. At 0800 Perdue contacted Talkeetna to inform them that the situation had been resolved. By 0820 Dong had treated and released Volkov but not before strongly discouraging Volkov and Nazar from executing their plan to attempt to summit from 14,200 feet with an alpine-style push.

Analysis

This situation had the potential for creating a very hazardous situation. This team chose to travel unroped through a section of the route known for its crevasses and the potential to fall into them. They did not stay together and they were clearly operating on a slim margin of personnel safety as evidenced by Volkov's frostbite. Nazar did admit during discussions with Perdue that they had made a mistake and should have stayed together. Volkov's expressing an interest in attempting to summit from 14,200 feet with minimal equipment is further indication of inexperience. It is also worth noting that VIP Ranger Dong was contacted later that same day by Volkov who requested to borrow a water bottle and indicated that the team had lost the handle to their only shovel. (Source: Ranger Margaret Perdue)

ABANDONMENT–CREATING A HAZARD
Alaska, Mount McKinley, West Buttress

Joseph Klopack (51) and his 15-year-old son Joseph, Jr. checked into the Talkeetna Ranger Station on June 3, where Ranger John Leonard briefed them. The pair flew to the Kahiltna Basecamp later that day, the starting point for their climb of Mt. McKinley. It appears that while in Talkeetna they met Dusan Golubic of the Slovak Republic who befriended the pair. The three joined up as a rope of three where they departed basecamp on June 3. They attempted to carry half their provisions all the way to 11,000 feet, but between 7,800 feet and 9,500 feet, Klopack Jr. experienced acute mountain sickness. Apparently they returned to base camp. Klopack, Jr. was left unsupervised at the Kahiltna Basecamp for four days while his father departed to climb the mountain. Klopack Jr. soloed (unroped) each day on extended glacier walks. Klopack Jr. flew off the mountain by himself on June 9. He traveled to Anchorage to stay with an acquaintance his father had met on the mountain. (Source: Ranger Roger Robinson)

Analysis

This report, while not complete, is included because of its unusual nature. We have not had a situation quite like this before. The behavior of the Klopacks, especially the father, was, to say the least, inappropriate. There was discussion as to whether to charge Mr. Klopack with violating the Alaska State Code, Chapter 51, which includes a section on "Endangering the welfare of a child in the first degree." Rangers Roger Robinson and Daryl Miller elected for a strong conversation with Mr. Klopack. (Source: Jed Williamson)

FALL ON ROCK–RAPPEL TECHNIQUE
Arizona, Windy Point

On August 31, Joaquin Fox (38) was climbing with several other people in the North Fin area west of Windy Point. He had reached the top of his climb when he fell 80 feet, still connected to his rope according to Pima County Sheriff's Deputy T.J. Price. Fox was unable to stop himself and neither could his belayer, Lori Elliott, the climbing partner who secured his rope. Fox hit the rocks below and tumbled, injuring his back and eye and possibly received other head injuries, Price said.

Crews from the Southern Arizona Rescue Association, the Mount Lemmon Fire District and Rural/Metro Fire Department helped in the rescue. Rescuers hiked to Fox, then hauled him up about 200 feet away from the climbing slope, then carried him a short distance to a saddle where the Department of Public Safety's Ranger helicopter was able to land. Fox was flown to University Medical Center about 3:45 p.m.

Analysis

Cody Tye and Ryan Fitzgerald were climbing nearby when Fox fell. At first, Tye said, it seemed like Fox was doing a fast rappel, but then he shouted "Stop!" The friction of the rope helped to slow Fox, but the fall still appeared potentially devastating, Fitzgerald said. "I actually thought he was going to be dead." Tye called Fox a "real experienced, sharp climber..." (Source: Eric Swedlund, *Tucson Arizona Star*)

(Editor's Note: This was the only report received from Arizona this year. No other details were available.)

FALL ON ROCK–PROTECTION FAILED, INADEQUATE PROTECTION
California, Yosemite Valley, El Capitan

On May 4, Cam McKenzie (26) and I, Scott Ring (25), started up our fixed lines on the Zodiac route (VI 5.7 A2) on El Capitan. We picked up our haul bags where we'd stashed them at the top of pitch three and continued on, hoping to spend the night at the top of pitch seven. We each had a decade of climbing experience and had done a few shorter walls, but this was our first El Cap route.

By early evening we'd finished pitch six, and I was starting the seventh. I traversed left and up for a ways on mixed free and aid, then the pitch turned upward to follow the right side of the Black Tower. At the point where it turned, I placed a solid stopper for aid. A couple of moves later, however, I looked down and realized that the direction change might pull out that stopper, upward, if there were tension in the rope. I had great cams in above the stopper so I decided to keep going.

Eventually I was standing on the top of the Tower with a Camalot about two feet below my feet. The next placement was a fixed copperhead just above me. The climbing above the Tower is rated C3RF; this means hard aid on fixed gear, with the potential for a dangerous fall because of ledges below. I'd climbed C3+ before. It was right at my limit, and I didn't like the looks of that head. I stood there for a long time, searching for something else. The topo showed a couple of bolts right there. Even a halfway decent bolt would get me by the head, so I looked all over, but there was none to be found. A crack right next to the fixed head was flaring, totally blown out, and would not accept my cam. Although I thought it might take a sawed off angle, I wanted to do this clean, so I decided to go with the head and try to reach the next piece of fixed gear. First I gave the head a couple of delicate bounces, with one foot balancing on top of the Tower. I didn't see any movement, so I stepped up. I had just reached my second to last step, maybe three feet above the Tower, when the head blew.

I hit the Tower with my feet, bounced off and spun sideways. I was falling on my right side, facing the rock, with my head toward Cam, who was 15–20 feet down and to the right. I remember my helmet taking a few hits along the way. Below me, about even with Cam, was a detached flake. I fell 10–15 feet and scored a direct hit on the flake with my right hip—the wing of the pelvis, where your pants ride. It flipped me upside down because I had a big aid rack on my chest harness.

The rope came tight right away and I only fell another couple of feet. The Camalot at the top of the Tower and the pieces just below it held, but the stopper lower in the corner—the one I'd been concerned about—pulled out. This allowed the rope to take a shorter path, adding maybe three feet of slack to the system. I might have hit more gently, or not at all, if I had taken more care with that placement.

The first thing I recall is my vision going black and white and feeling the shriek of pain in my hip. I knew I was hurt, though I didn't know what the injury was. I wanted to right myself, so I focused on clipping in my chest harness. Cam was repeatedly yelling, "Are you OK?" but at the time I couldn't talk—I just wanted to clip myself in. Then I told her I was OK. I never did lose consciousness, but I felt like I was right at the verge. Finally, Cam lowered me and I cleaned a couple of pieces on the traverse as I swung over to the belay. I was hoping it was something I could shake off. At the belay ledge I realized that I couldn't put any weight on my right side—it was really tender—and I sat there leaning to the left.

It was close to sunset and I first thought, 'OK, let's just set up the portaledge here and call it a night.' Cam was rearranging everything so that we would have room for the ledge. But then I felt my back. It was swelling really fast, between my spine and my right hip. That scared me. We talked about it and decided to go down.

A descent from the top of pitch six, where we were, was pretty straight forward: We could make one rappel to the top of pitch four on double ropes. From there, our two 60-meter ropes, tied end-to-end, would reach the ground. We'd take our gear with us and leave the ropes in place for friends to retrieve. I felt I could get myself to the base, but there was no way I'd get down a quarter mile of talus boulders by myself. We had our cell phone, so I called a friend who lives in the park and he notified the Park Service.

Cam took the haul bag, the hardware rack, and the portaledge, and went down to pitch four, so I had only myself to manage. I kept a little bit of gear to clip in if I needed it. We had each rigged two descenders to make changeovers easier—at a knot we'd rig one descender below the knot, then de-rig the one above it. I clipped both of mine to my big-wall chest harness and backed that harness up to my seat harness. The chest harness fit really well and kept most of the weight off my hips. My right leg just hanging there was killing me, but I supported it by clipping the loop in the back of my shoe to my harness. This relieved a lot of the pain, and I was able to brace myself with my good leg on the wall.

It was totally dark when I got to pitch four, where Cam was waiting. We tied the two lines together, anchored one end, and tossed them off. The cliff was steep enough there that they hung away from the wall. We knew how to pass knots while hanging on the rope, but I felt like I wanted something solid to stabilize myself in case I needed it. So Cam's main objective as she rappelled was to keep the rope close to the wall. She would look for suitable places to tie it off until we were past the knot joining the ropes. Because of the way the Zodiac angles up and left, we were above the lower pitches of the Shortest Straw route. Cam rappelled from pitch four and found a belay station on Shortest Straw about 30 meters down, where she anchored the line. I joined her there and tied myself off, then she went on down another 30 meters to the joining knot.

The Shortest Straw anchor was a hanging station with a couple of bolts. A solo climber was somewhere in the dark above me, and all his gear was hanging from the bolts. I clipped off short and tried to stand on his haul bag and to position myself with an etrier, but it hurt a lot even to use my good leg so I mostly weighted my chest harness. Then I relaxed as much as I could and looked at the stars a lot. Meanwhile, Cam was swinging around 30 meters below. She found a cluster of gear—not at an anchor, but just fixed along the pitch—and managed to clove-hitch the rope there, right next to the joining knot.

By this time rescuers on the ground were yelling up to Cam. They had good intentions, trying to find out what was going on, but Cam needed to concentrate on what she had to do and she finally had to ask the rescuers to give her a moment

Up at the Shortest Straw anchor, I couldn't hear what they were saying and everything seemed to take forever and in my little bubble I was thinking, "Ow, hurry up!"

Cam had the haul bag on her rappel loop, so it was quite heavy for her when she was off rappel at the fixed gear. On rappel, its weight was on the descender, but passing the knot was still quite a hassle for her. She finally got to the ground and yelled up at me to come down.

With the rope clipped off I was able to rappel right to the fixed pieces, and Cam had left some slings there for me to grab. It was still a bit overhanging. As before, I clipped in an etrier for my good foot and used it to un-weight the rope when I needed to; I hung off my chest harness the rest of the time. But I was swinging around so it was tricky and every little move was another "Ow!"

I set up the descender below the knot, transferred my weight, released the rope from the wall, and swung out a couple of feet. Then I went straight to the ground, or rather, into the arms of the rescue team, who helped me into a litter. From the time of my fall it had taken me three hours to go down three rope-lengths.

They started an IV and morphine immediately and carried me straight down the talus. It was 2:00 a.m. by the time we got to the road. I was flown to Modesto where it took a CAT scan to discover that I'd broken the pubic ramus in my pelvis. The weird thing was that the huge swelling wasn't blood, but lymph, as though I'd ruptured a lymph duct. They released me that day and Cam drove me home in the van, flat on my back, all doped up. I'm 100 percent healed now, several months later, and back on the rock.

Analysis

In hindsight I should have dug out the hammer and tried a piton instead of relying on a head I didn't trust. I also should have trusted my judgment and improved that corner piece that pulled. That may have made the difference in my injury. Being competent on the ropes helped a lot to get us down, but I think our tiny headlamps would have been a problem if we'd had to see farther to spot anchors, so I also carry a longer-range model now. (Source: Scott Ring and John Dill, NPS Ranger, Yosemite National Park)

FALL ON ROCK, INADEQUATE PROTECTION, NO HARD HAT
California, Yosemite Valley, Lower Cathedral Rock

On May 21, Chris Hampson (28) and Sibylle Hechtel (52) teamed up to climb Overhang Bypass on Lower Cathedral Rock. The route is approximately six pitches, originally rated 5.6 but considered more difficult since a large block fell from the crux a number of years ago, creating a mandatory 5.8/5.9 mantle. Their plan was to climb the route and top-rope Overhang Overpass, a 5.11 crack accessible from the upper section of Overhang Bypass.

Both Chris and Sibylle had climbed extensively in Yosemite, Chris having spent the last month climbing full time in the Valley, and Sibylle having decades of Yosemite experience under her belt. This was their second route together, and it was well within their abilities.

Chris led the first pitch up easy climbing without placing any protection. Sibylle led the second pitch, to the base of the Hog Trough. The Trough is a system of ledges traversing up and left for just over 100 feet to where the route turns upward through the crux mantle. After this move, the pitch turns back right through moderate but loose terrain.

Chris headed up the Trough and clipped the rope through protection about 30 feet beyond the belay. After another 60 feet or so of easy climbing, he passed a tree, climbing between the tree and the wall so that his rope ran behind its trunk. Though he did not clip his rope to the tree, by climbing behind it he created a "natural" piece of protection. The crux mantle is 15-20 feet beyond this tree, and as Chris continued up the ledges toward the mantle, he climbed out of Sibylle's view.

A few minutes later Sibylle heard Chris yell and felt the rope jerk tight under the force of a fall. She still could not see him from her belay, and her own yells brought no answer, but she could feel his weight on the rope. Within five minutes or so, while Sibylle was calling to Chris, Bob Jensen arrived, having soloed the lower section of the route. After learning what had happened, Bob continued up the Trough to the tree. From there he could just see Chris, hanging at least fifty feet below, his rope having caught around the tree's trunk. When Bob called down to him, Chris answered in a disoriented manner and said that he could not see. Without any gear to reach him, Bob soloed back down the route and went for help while Sibylle escaped the anchor and climbed up to the tree to communicate with Chris. When Bob left it was about 11:30 a.m., roughly fifteen or twenty minutes after Chris's accident. Over the next hour Chris's condition deteriorated until Sibylle could only hear an occasional yell or moan from below.

Bob reached the rescue office in Yosemite Valley about forty five minutes later. After hearing the situation, Ranger Keith Lober and I immediately headed for the route while a larger group geared up to follow. We arrived at Lower Cathedral Rock about 12:45 and saw Chris through binoculars. He was hanging by his rope in a corner, about 70 feet below the tree, sitting upright and moving his arms. Keith and I reached Sibylle at the top of the Hog Trough by approximately 1:30 p.m. Unfortunately no quick, adequate protection was available where we needed it, and the tree that had caught Chris's fall appeared far from solid, so we immediately began drilling bolt anchors.

Five minutes before we reached Sibylle, our spotter, watching through a telescope from across the Valley, radioed that Chris had stopped moving and was now slumped over backwards. By the time we reached him about twenty minutes later (but almost three hours after the fall) he was beyond resuscitation. We are not certain what injury killed him, but it was probably a combination of head and chest trauma, perhaps with additional physiological stress from hanging for so long in his harness.

Analysis

Chris was familiar with Yosemite's rock and comfortable leading well beyond the level of this route. We don't know what caused his fall, but we do know a couple of things that made it longer and more damaging than it might have been.

Based on the amount of rope between Chris and the tree that caught him, he may have fallen over a hundred feet. Once he was out of Sibylle's view, the time that passed and the rope she fed out suggest that he climbed beyond the crux mantle into the moderate terrain above. He may have been 50–60 feet beyond the tree when something went wrong.

The tree may have been Chris's last piece of protection. We did find a single stopper clipped to the rope immediately above his harness, but details suggest that he clipped this piece to the rope after his fall in order to secure his backpack—which we found hanging from the same carabiner.

Protecting the mantle well is difficult though possible, and Chris either ignored or missed a fixed piton just past the tree. Gear options in the moderate terrain above are also sparse, though protection is available. Whether he fell at the crux or 40 feet beyond, the length of that fall clearly would have been less had he placed additional protection.

In addition to potentially "running it out" on terrain where he felt comfortable, Chris was also not wearing a helmet. The crux is steep, but the overall angle of the route is less than vertical, and Chris likely hit several ledges as he tumbled down the wall. Though a helmet might not have saved his life, it certainly would have improved the odds. (Source: Lincoln Else, NPS Ranger, Yosemite National Park)

FALL ON ROCK
California, Yosemite Valley, Manure Pile Buttress

On May 23, Irene Appelbaum (41) and Ricardo Lagos (28) climbed the Nutcracker (five pitches, 5.8) on Manure Pile Buttress, with Ricardo taking all the leads. On the final pitch, he placed a small cam just above the crux 5.8 mantle and did the move. He then finished the remaining 80–100 foot slab, setting one more cam along the way.

At the top, Ricardo rigged his anchor ten feet back from the edge but sat at the lip so that he could talk with Irene. He belayed her through a Reverso (in autolock mode) clipped to the anchor. He kept a fairly tight rope, with just a little slack. He felt Irene come quickly up the short slab at the start of the pitch, then slow down at the corner leading to the mantle. When he felt her move up again, he lifted the rope a foot or two to pull in the slack, and just as he started to pull the slack through the Reverso, she fell. There was no significant slippage through the belay.

The corner is steep and perhaps eight or ten feet high, with the mantle as its exit move. Except for a narrow ledge a couple of feet above the slab, footholds are scarce until one passes the mantle. Although Irene had climbed it successfully in the past, this time she was having trouble with the crux. She went up and down a few times and finally decided to grab the sling on the small cam. She was hanging on to the cam when her feet slipped.

She remembers her left foot hitting something on the wall almost immediately and then hearing several "pops" as she fell slowly for a short distance—no tumbling, just a straightforward, feet-first, top-rope fall. She remained where she was, supported by the rope, with her right foot on a tiny nubbin and holding her left foot out in front of her, until she was rescued.

Despite his position at the edge, Ricardo could not communicate with her. After several minutes with no action on the rope, he realized something must be wrong and that he needed to rappel to within earshot. Since Irene was roughly 100 feet below the anchor, he assumed the other half of his 200-foot rope would be able to get him close. He left the Reverso locked off at the anchor and tied the rope off to the anchor on the belayer's side of the Reverso. This would back up Irene's belay and also anchor his rappel.

Since his Reverso was in the belay system, he rappelled with a carabiner wrap—trying this for the first time. (He had brought a spare belay/descent device on the climb but, assuming the climb was over, had left it and several other items with Irene when he led the final pitch.) He remained tied to his end of the rope, but had no prusik for a safety. As he descended, twists built up in the rope from the carabiner wrap. Since the end of the rope was tied to him, there was nowhere for the twists to go and they finally stopped his progress just above the mantle. He did not think to tie in short and drop the end to get the twists out, but at least he was now within talking distance.

After discussing and then discarding the possibility of getting Irene to the top, he decided to climb out and go for help. The summit slabs are fairly easy, so he was able to hand-over-hand—again without prusik safety—back up the rope to his anchor. He then hiked down to the base of the wall, where he asked someone with a cell phone to call 911. The rescue team got a medic to Irene within an hour and lowered her in a litter 600 feet to the ground with the medic attending. Two hours elapsed from the time the 911 call was received until Irene was in the ambulance. She was diagnosed with a bi-malleolar fracture dislocation of her left ankle that required surgery, lots of hardware, and a bone graft to repair.

Analysis

Following a pitch is usually pretty safe, but after a long lead the inherent stretch and slack in the system can sometimes result in a risky fall. Irene probably fell five or six feet, nearly back to the slab—not much, and not fast, but enough for the right kind of blow to do the damage. (In fact we see many sprained and broken ankles even from simple stumbles on the trail.) So don't hesitate to ask for a snug belay when you are challenged by the move.

Ricardo had been climbing six months and he admits that he lacked some of the knowledge and gear for safely getting down to Irene and then back to the summit. This is not a self-rescue text, but here are a few suggestions:

If you need your belay device and it's tied up in the system, first anchor the belay line with a prusik in front of the device, then tie the rope off behind it, allowing enough slack to remove the device. If your rappel is stopped by kinks in the rope, tie off the descender or tie in short, then untie your end of the rope and shake out the twists. Know how to use several rappel rigs—Munter, carabiner brake, etc. Know the uses and limitations of prusiks when rappelling and ascending the line, and how to tie in short. Finally, know how to assist your partner to the summit or to lower her to the base—if the injury and terrain allow. These skills may get you out of trouble in a more remote and more serious environment. (Source: John Dill, NPS Ranger, Yosemite National Park.)

FALL ON ROCK–INAPPROPRIATE DESCENT TECHNIQUE, OFF ROUTE, EXCEEDING ABILITIES
California, Yosemite National Park, Tenaya Canyon

On the morning of June 20, I, Graham (18), set out from Tenaya Lake for a solo cross-country day hike to Yosemite Valley via Tenaya Canyon. I had been climbing in the park for about a week on this, my first visit, and had heard about the route from Park Service friends. The terrain is mostly second/third class, along Tenaya Creek in the bottom of the canyon. A couple of rappels are necessary for most parties, but an acquaintance in the park, familiar with the canyon, described his route for me, saying that I might have no need for a rope if I stayed to the right of the creek. I did bring a rope, but no hardware or helmet—I wanted to keep my pack light, and I'd heard that all the rappels were on slabs, so I figured I could hand-over-hand down the rope on anything I might unintentionally encounter. I also brought a few typical day-hiking items and threw in my cell phone for good measure.

After a few hours of hiking down the canyon on fairly straightforward terrain, the creek abruptly dropped over a waterfall into a narrow gorge 50-75 feet deep. I'd been told about a gorge, but I had no idea it would be so difficult. A steep rappel would get me to the creek bed below; however, I couldn't see far enough downstream to determine if there was a way out, so I decided to stay out of the gorge and continue looking for the third-class route I'd been told I might find.

I worked my way up the side of the canyon on river right and continued downstream, bushwhacking through manzanita, several hundred feet above the creek. Then the terrain led me down slabs into a small drainage that, like the main creek had earlier, dropped off the edge of a vertical cliff. From my vantage point, it was clear that if I could get to the bottom of the cliff, a scramble would take me back to Tenaya Creek, and a hike of a couple miles would get me to the Valley. I spent an hour or two looking around for an alternative way down, but descending the cliff seemed to be my best option.

I doubled my rope around a tree near the edge, grabbed hold of it, and looked over. The rope clearly didn't reach the bottom, but it did just reach a slab 75 feet below me that angled down to a shallow, rocky pool of water on a broad ledge. I judged that I could hand-over-hand down to the end of the rope and onto the slab, then climb down to the ledge. Once on the ledge, the rest would be easy.

I went down the rope with hands and feet, nothing else securing me. I had done hand-over-hand descents on large drops many times before and, although this one was steeper, even overhanging, I felt completely comfortable going over the edge. I was almost to the slab when I noticed the nature of the rope changing. The water dripping off the edge above was soaking the rope. Instead of one hand holding fast while I moved the other, it would slip an inch. I started to move faster, trying to keep pace with the slippage. When I was five or ten feet from the end of the rope and only five feet from the slab, I completely lost my grip and slid down and off the rope onto the slab. I tumbled down the slab, bouncing hard two or three times, and into the pool. I estimated the fall at about 40 feet, but my rescuers later told me it was closer to 80 feet.

I remember opening my eyes after I landed and thinking, "Holy shit, I fell! Holy shit, I'm OK!" I touched my head and saw that I was bleeding. That was all I felt initially, but when I stood up to walk away I was hit with excruciating pain in my right leg. I looked down and saw that it was pointing in the wrong direction, so I crawled out of the water about 20 feet to a dry section and conceded defeat.

My cell phone had miraculously survived the fall and the pool of water, so I tried calling 911 and I got a reply. I was only able to give the rangers a rough idea of where I was, but they spotted me from the park helicopter pretty quickly. Then they managed to find a landing spot several hundred yards away in the canyon bottom and two medics scrambled up to my ledge. After they worked on me a while, a second helicopter (California. Highway Patrol) hoisted me and flew me to the Valley, where I was transferred to an air ambulance for the trip to a hospital in Modesto. The whole top of my right femur was broken apart, my pelvis was cracked, and I had an L4 compression fracture. At this point, nine months later, I have been cleared to do whatever activities I choose, but I'll probably lay off the contact sports a little longer.

Analysis

This was the most traumatic thing that has ever occurred to me, mostly because I did it to myself. I still have dreams about it, and the accident is never far from my mind. I have never been as embarrassed as when I had to call for help and put people in danger for my sake. I almost didn't call for that reason. I can hardly be classed as a beginner. I've had the benefit of 18 years of outdoor education from my family, have been climbing my whole life, and have had extensive canyoneering experience elsewhere. It sounds crazy even to me, now, but I was really comfortable going down hand-over-hand. It was standard procedure back home, but on a cliff this steep and this high it was a dumb thing to do. I could easily have turned around and hiked back to Tenaya Lake, even if I had had to spend the night en route. But the greatest lesson learned was humility. I needed a big slap in the face because I was getting way too cocky with my climbing. I definitely got a BIG slap in the face.

Obviously once you are out there—on trail or off—you have to use your own judgment every step of the way. The advice from Graham's friends may have been correct, but it was insufficiently detailed to keep him on track in such rough country, and he had actually wandered off route.

A map will sometimes help, but it, too, will lack the necessary resolution. Also, if you are going to put a rope in your pack, take the gear to go down it safely. Add to this some prusiks and lightweight foot loops for ascending your line again if you find yourself at a dead end. Graham would hardly have noticed the weight of this gear in his daypack, and it would have been far cheaper than all those helicopters and hospital bills. Tenaya Canyon has been the scene of many strandings, injuries, and fatalities, all involving parties without the skills and/or gear for the terrain. (Source: Graham and John Dill, NPS Ranger, Yosemite National Park)

(Editor's Note: While not a climbing accident, this is a good example of a hiking situation that turned into a climbing problem.)

FALL ON ROCK, RAPPEL ANCHOR FAILED
California, Yosemite National Park, Cathedral Peak

On July 2, Aaron (28), Mark (48), Chad (28), and Brian (49) started up the West Pillar of Eichorn Pinnacle (five pitches, 5.9 or 5.10b). Brian was unable to manage the first pitch, so he chose to wait at the base while Aaron, Mark, and Chad finished the route. After climbing the first pitch and starting the others decided that rather than keeping Brian waiting, they would rappel off, join Brian, and go cragging elsewhere.

Aaron stopped halfway up the second pitch, established an anchor, and brought up Mark and Chad. The anchor was built from his own gear, so he was reluctant to leave it behind when they descended. He spotted a cluster of slings about 25 feet further up the pitch and climbed up to a small ledge just below them, for a look. He found three slings sticking out of a finger-crack, with a screw link and a carabiner attached to them. They had almost certainly been set up and used for rappels, and from what he could see, they were in good condition. He spread the slings apart and peered into the crack. The slings were wedged so deep that he had difficulty seeing the exact lay-out, but they appeared to be tied around a constriction where the two sides of the crack seemed to come together. He built a temporary anchor of his own a couple of feet below the slings and clipped himself to it. Backed up by that anchor, he rigged his ropes through the link and the carabiner on the slings and bounce-tested the slings as though he were on rappel. They seemed solid, so he decided to use them to anchor the party's first rappel. He pulled his temporary anchor and, with the slings as his rappel anchor, rappelled 25 feet to rejoin Mark and Chad at their belay.

From that point they would need to make two rappels to the ground. The first would be anchored through the slings above, so Aaron left the ropes in place. Mark was eager to rappel first and set up the next station. He got on rappel and worked his way out a few feet to the right of the route, flipping the ropes to the right as he went, to keep them out of the main crack. As Mark descended around a corner and out of sight, Aaron turned his attention to other chores. A minute later he heard a "pop!", like a gunshot, up at the rappel anchor, and a yell from Chad. Aaron turned around to see Mark fall to the ground, 250 feet below, followed by the ropes and the anchor slings.

Brian, a physician, was waiting at the base and scrambled over to Mark. He noticed immediately that Mark had suffered fatal trauma and was without a pulse. He tried CPR nevertheless, but realized the futility and finally gave up.

The ropes had hung up on the cliff 120 feet below Aaron and Chad, but Aaron was able to climb down to them by protecting himself with cams on long slings and back-cleaning as he went. He rigged an anchor and rappelled to the ground, where Brian confirmed that Mark was dead. Aaron then climbed up to Chad, with Brian belaying, and made sure that Chad got down safely. Then Aaron hiked out and notified the NPS. Rangers recovered Mark's body that evening.

Analysis

When examined by the NPS on the afternoon of the accident, the rappel slings and hardware were intact—no broken or untied slings. An NPS team climbed to the site of the failed anchors the next day and examined the crack, but they were unable to determine exactly where and how the slings had been rigged. They did find one constriction in the crack that at first appeared to be a complete closure, however a more careful inspection showed it to be open enough that an anchor built there could fail. The team did not have the original rappel slings at that time, so they were unable to try to recreate the original anchor. Aaron had not been sure that the slings had actually been arranged as he remembered them, and other rigging possibilities existed at the site, based on dimensions of the slings and features of the rock. Aaron also remembers that there was a horn above this point just out of view that could have been used as well.

Aaron had noticed no movement as he tested the slings, but Mark weighed over 200 pounds and he may have added extra stress to the system as he flipped the already-loaded ropes to the right. Directionality may have been a factor, but any change in direction at the rappel slings due to Mark's movements should have been fairly small, given his distance below them. Both Aaron and Mark had been climbing for years and certainly knew how to rig anchors and how to rappel.

Of course we can advise that all rappelling be done gently, but much more important is that the anchor be secure. Every anchor must be completely inspected visually. If you can't see the whole anchor, that's where the problem is apt to be—rock-abraded, rat-chewed, loose knot, false constriction, etc. Second, don't hesitate to add a sling of your own. In the case at hand, a horn two or three feet above the anchor would have accepted a sling as a back up. Finally, don't assume that an anchor is safe just because other parties have used it without incident, even if recently. (Source: John Dill, NPS Ranger, Yosemite National Park)

STRANDED–OFF ROUTE, WEATHER, INADEQUATE CLOTHING AND EQUIPMENT, EXCEEDING ABILITIES
California, Tuolumne Meadows, Fairview Dome

On July 27, Randy Popkin (46) and his son, Cameron (16), climbed the Regular Route on Fairview Dome. They got to the base at 7:00 a.m. to allow plenty of time for the route, but a party of four was already there. Waiting for the larger party to clear the second pitch cost the Popkins 45 minutes, and then another hour on the third. The party of four ultimately pulled ahead, but the Popkins then lost more time allowing a faster party to pass. Randy and Cameron were having no problems with the technical difficulty of the climb, but they were getting a lesson in the realities of a long and popular route.

Finally, high on the face, where the route traverses to the right to the final fourth-class pitches, they missed the turn and continued straight up. By the time they realized their error and had rappelled back to their previous belay, another 45 minutes had gone by. By now it was nearing dusk, and Randy knew they would not get off. They reached the fourth-class section and ran up it as fast as they could, but they had no lights, and darkness stopped them 100 feet from the top.

The forecast had been good—no storms in sight—and the day had been excellent, but clouds began to build up in the late afternoon. At dusk it began to rain and hail, with lightning in the distance. Randy was somewhat protected with light nylon pants and a fleece-lined Goretex jacket, but Cameron had only shorts and a cotton long-sleeve sweatshirt. Luckily the precipitation never became heavy, and they found a decent ledge with an overhang that allowed partial shelter.

Their water and food had lasted all day, but now it was gone. They did, however, have a Family Band radio, and Randy's wife—who had already notified the NPS that they were overdue—was able to contact them from the road at about midnight. Randy initially figured they would sit it out, but he changed his mind when he realized that Cameron was getting cold.

The Park Service was also concerned that a second thunderstorm was forming, so they sent two members of the rescue team to the top of Fairview. They were able to rappel to the Popkins and belay them to the summit. Everyone walked out to the road a little before 6:00 a.m., just as the sun was coming up.

Analysis

Both had been climbing indoors and outdoors for the last two years and consistently followed 5.10. Cameron was not yet leading, but Randy had led a dozen or so single-pitch climbs at the 5.9 level. Neither had done a multi-pitch route without a guide, but a guide familiar with Randy's progress had suggested that he was ready to lead Fairview. The guide felt Randy was ready to lead the route, and he was right, as the climbing was never an issue. But a new leader and a non-leader make a pretty weak team if anything serious happens, and the guide probably assumed that Randy would include an experienced climber in the party.

Here's a short list of common practices: Don't trust the weather forecast, especially in the high country. Depending on the route, your skill level, and your style, take headlamps, warm clothes (including hats), and lightweight rain gear. Also consider a spare, lightweight rope so that you can make full-pitch rappels without leaving your entire rack behind. A cell phone or FRS radio (and someone on the other end) is also a good idea. But it's no substitute for preparation and ability. Expect delays—almost everyone we rescue because of darkness or storm blames heavy traffic or the lack of street signs. Check your progress and be realistic. Adverse conditions are no big deal if you're equipped to sit the situation out. Otherwise you should retreat while you're able. (Source: John Dill, NPS Ranger, Yosemite National Park)

FALL ON ROCK, WEATHER
California, Tuolumne Meadows, Daff Dome

On July 29, Hope Wolf (28), an instructor for the Yosemite Mountaineering School, was leading a group of six clients back from a day's climbing at Daff Dome when they were caught by a mid-afternoon downpour. In similar weather a week earlier, the trail to the road down the dirt gully had become so full of running water that it was unsafe to hike. Furthermore, the group would have done significant damage to the wet soil, so Hope had taken her clients down the alternate route on low-angle granite slabs. Faced with the same conditions, she chose the slabs again.

The rock was slick and two or three of the group had slipped and fallen. Mark Bayless slipped once, but Hope stopped him. A few feet further, just before a two-foot drop-off, Mark slipped again and went down. Hope turned to stop him, but they were so close together that he caught her off balance and carried her off the drop. The slide would ordinarily have been harmless, but her right foot stopped in a twisted position and stayed there as she kept going. The momentum of her own body, her 50-pound pack, and Mark's 200 pounds on top of that, gave her ankle no chance. When she came to a stop she looked down to see the sole of her right shoe staring up at her and an ankle bone trying to poke through the skin.

Hope called back to the class that she was hurt and told everyone to stop, then she had them descend one at a time. Co-instructor Grant Hiskes verified that the nerve function and circulation in her foot was intact. While someone went for help, Grant tried to splint the leg as he found it, but the deformity got in the way and pressure of the bone under the skin caused too much pain.

The NPS rescue team began arriving about 30 minutes after the accident. With the help of a little morphine, Duane Grego, an NPS paramedic, was able to realign the dislocated bones and splint the ankle. The team carried

Hope, in a litter, the remaining 300 feet to the road. She was transported by ambulance to Mammoth Hospital, where three fractures in the ankle were repaired.

Analysis

Both Hope and the rangers at the scene agree that most parties would not use a belay on such a low-angle slab. (There were no anchors available, anyway.) However, an accident like this one would be a major logistical hassle if it were ten miles in the backcountry, and no one wants to put up with several months of physical therapy. This incident is a reminder to stay alert, even on the easy stuff. (Source: John Dill, NPS Ranger, Yosemite National Park)

(Editor's Note: Again, a hiking situation that turned into the need for climbing technique.)

FALL ON ROCK–DISLODGED ROCK, OFF ROUTE, FATIGUE
California, Sierra Nevada, Clyde Minaret

On Saturday, August 16th, Justin Schwartz of Belmont, CA, and Steve Sosa, of Los Angeles, CA, set off to climb the South Face of 12,300-foot Clyde Minaret. Justin and Steve knew one another well, having been a climbing team for more than 20 years, and having spent their summer youth together in Yosemite Valley.

The summit ridge is a knife-edge of loose stone blocks leading to near vertical drops of 1500 feet or more on either side. Upon descending 50 feet off the summit, Justin lost his footing and dislodged a large stone block onto himself and tumbled 20 feet down the cliff landing on a narrow ledge. Pain seared his legs and arm, and he could not move. It was 5:30 p.m., with nightfall at 7:45, little water, and no bivouac gear or extra clothing.

Steve was able to contact emergency dispatch in Madeira County via cellular phone, and by 11:30 that night, Mono County Mountain SAR mounted a rescue.

Early Sunday morning, the team went with a Black Hawk helicopter crew from the Sacramento Air National Guard to assess the feasibility of rescue. With the helicopter hovering only a few feet from the rocky summit, the stranded climbers were raised on a hoist and returned to the Mammoth Lakes Airport where local paramedics met them.

Justin suffered a fractured left hip, fractured right lower leg, deep lacerations to his left shin, minor lacerations and contusions to his left arm and hand, and a severely sprained right ankle.

Analysis

There is considerable loose rock and rockfall hazard in the Minarets, with the final pitches and summit ridge being quite loose, so climbers should be especially cautious. Steve and Justin were somewhat vague about the descent route. It is a common mistake on Clyde Minaret for climbers to attempt to descend to the left (south) too soon, rather than continuing on the ridge to the northwest for several hundred feet. Lastly, Steve and Justin started the Grade IV route at 8:00 a.m., and it is possible that a late start, fatigue and anxiety to move quickly were contributing factors. (Source: Craig Knoche –Mono County Mountain SAR)

FALL ON ROCK, PROTECTION PULLED OUT, INEXPERIENCE
California, Yosemite Valley, Sunnyside Bench, Jam Crack

On September 11, Kristen Shive (26) was attempting to lead Jam Crack. She fell after placing a second piece of protection on the first pitch. The protection held, then held again on her second fall. On the third attempt, she fell again and the protection came out. She fell to the ground, landing on her feet, but sustained an angulated fracture of her right ankle.

Analysis

First and foremost, I don't believe I had much business leading Jam Crack at that point, or leading trad at all. I had been climbing (not intensely) for a little over a year—and even then I knew that sport climbing would be better to start with. But I did a lot of climbing after work in the Valley and didn't really have that option. So my impatience, combined with support from my climbing partner lead me to plunge in a little before my skill level was there.

Anyway, I had led only two 5.6 routes, and only decided to try my hand at Jam Crack because I had followed it so many times I felt like I could do it in my sleep. I'm sure that's an exaggeration, but I was really, really comfortable on that route and felt like I knew it and so might do better there than on a 5.6 I didn't know so well.

And the details from there on are rather simple. I headed up the route and I had only placed my second piece (and to be honest it probably would have been my first, but I was sticking in extra to get comfortable placing pieces), when I fell on it. It held, and I remember thinking how weird it was that I fell there—not a tricky spot for even my skill level. I also remember thinking "Great, it's solid, I placed it well." Anyway I tried again and the same thing happened. (This is where I get embarrassed at my stupidity!). On the third try the piece pulled and I hit the ground. I wasn't aware of the simple rule that you should reset a piece if you fall on it.

If you're at all interested in the retrospect thoughts of a new and thoughtless (at the time) climber it would be this—I would wait and gain more experience and skills before trying to lead, trad especially. I would listen to my body. While leading is always far harder than following, the fact that I was having so much trouble so early (three tries, not 15 feet up the route) on something I've been so comfortable on, should have been a sign. It was after work, and I'd been working long hours on fires and hiking hard. My body wasn't up to it and I ignored it. And while I take full responsibility for what happened, I would start leading with someone who has more experience as well. My partner had not led too terribly much more than I had. (Source: Kristen Shive)

FALL ON ROCK, INADEQUATE ANCHOR, INADEQUATE COMMUNICATION
California, Yosemite Valley, Ranger Rock

On the morning of September 11, E (25), N (27), and L (26) set out to climb the popular Nutcracker route in Yosemite Valley (5.8, five pitches). All three climbers were comfortable leading traditional routes at this level, and they reached the top of the third pitch without any problems. The party was leading with two 9-mm ropes, belaying each follower separately.

After leading the third pitch, N established a three-piece anchor at a small sloping ledge. (For those who know the route, he chose to take the right-hand variation following the crack, instead of face-climbing to the small tree up and left.) After equalizing his anchor with webbing, N secured himself directly to the webbing's "power-point" with a locking carabiner on his harness. Though not a true hanging belay, the angle of the wall was steep enough that he likely weighted the anchor at least partially. L then followed the pitch on the first rope and climbed slightly past N to a small ledge above and to his right. She was clipped to the anchor's power point with a long runner and a locking carabiner, yet she was out of the way and in position to lead the next pitch. Then N belayed E up on the second rope.

When he arrived at the anchor, E positioned himself slightly below and left of N, securing himself to the power point with a locking carabiner on a runner girth-hitched to his harness. At this point all three climbers were clipped into the same power-point, each with a single locking carabiner. After some discussion they decided that E should untie from his rope and pass his end to L; she had the first rope already, but needed the second one in order to lead the next pitch on a pair. N could have untied from his end of the second rope, but it was stacked such that using E's end would avoid a rope tangle. Before untying himself from the rope, E attached himself to the power point with a second locking carabiner on a second runner girth-hitched to his harness. Both L and N remember watching E clip this second runner to the anchor, and both heard his comment that he wanted a backup "just to be safe."

Once she was ready to lead the next pitch, L asked N to put her on belay and to unclip her locking carabiner from the anchor. N used his left hand to keep L on belay, while he unclipped what he believed to be her locking carabiner with his right. The next thing both L and N remember is seeing E tumble 250 feet down the rock face to the ground.

Analysis

As for the cause of this incident, it is apparent that something went wrong in one of the most basic climbing processes. The obvious questions are: Did N accidentally unclip E from the anchor? Even if he did, what happened to E's second clip-in point? And why did E fall, at that same moment?

Many of us have become unclipped at anchors sometimes accidentally, and sometimes intentionally to "save time" and because it's "only for a minute." Regardless of the cause, this accident underscores the importance of backup attachment points, and also the importance of communication when climbing in a team: "Does my partner's rigging—as well as my own—look OK? Does my partner know I'm unclipping one of my anchor points? Is this the right carabiner? Are we following the same plan?" The more people there are in a system, the more potential there is for confusion.

Accidents like this are more common than one might think. In Yosemite, up to 40 percent of all climbing fatalities over the last 30 years have been due to failures to maintain the integrity of the anchor chain, whether ascending a rope, rappelling or just waiting at the belay. (Source: Lincoln Else, NPS Ranger, Yosemite National Park)

(Ediotor's Note: The climbers wished not to have their names used.)

DEHYDRATION–INADEQUATE WATER, WEATHER
California, Yosemite Valley, El Capitan

On September 22, Mark Gunlogson (41) and I, Micha Miller (41), started up New Dawn wall (VI 5.8 A3) on El Captain. The weather before our ascent had been unseasonably warm (low 90's), with cooler temperatures forecast for the coming week. We considered waiting for the better conditions but were on a tight schedule and wanted to get started on the route. We planned on taking seven days. Knowing how critical water would be, we each had three quarts readily available for the first day, and five additional gallons per person, packed away in our two haul bags, for the next six days (3.3 quarts per person per day). In addition to what we figured was an ample supply of water, we were also prepared for fall storms, had a bolt kit, and, in short, were ready for any contingency—or so we thought.

Our goal for the 22nd was to climb three pitches and sleep at our high point, but it was very hot, and we moved more slowly than planned. We managed to finish our three pitches, but we left the haul bags at the top of pitch two and returned to the ground for more water. We slept at Curry Village, where we drank generous amounts of fruit juice and Gatorade to replenish what we had lost.

On the 23rd we left the ground with three more quarts each, giving us 3.8 quarts per person per day for the anticipated six days committed to the wall. It was slow going, with heavy bags and double hauls—the follower would have to wait until the first bag had been hauled, before he could release the second bag and start cleaning. Evening found us on Lay Lady Ledge (top of pitch seven, "Supertopo") after another hot day. We were tired and dehydrated, and we had drunk a bit more than our 3.8-quart ration.

On the 24th we climbed to Texas Flake (top of pitch 11). The temperature remained high, with not even the slightest hint of a breeze. Today, only our second continuous day on the wall, Mark's mouth became so parched—probably from breathing hard in the hot, dry air—that he gagged frequently, triggering dry heaves. He suffered this for the next four days.

On the 25th we completed the traverse to the top of pitch 13 of the Wall of Early Morning Light (pitch 14 of New Dawn). For more efficient hauling we had consolidated all of our stuff into one haul bag, but we could do nothing about the weather, which continued unchanged. This was Mark's tenth ascent of El Cap and my seventh, and neither of us had seen such a long period of both high temperatures and breezeless conditions on the wall. We had pressed on because we "knew" from experience that, at the very least, daily thermal winds would kick in, and that temperatures would drop as we got higher. However, this was proving not to be the case, and by this point we were thirsty all of the time. It was time to ration our water. We ate very little at meal times because we had brought dry food (not as much moist canned food as usual), and our thirst inhibited our hunger.

On the 26th (our fourth continuous day on the wall) we climbed three more pitches to Wino Tower and fixed one pitch. At Wino Tower (complete with broken wine bottle) we reviewed our progress and the water remaining. Our thirst continued to increase and we had involuntarily reduced our food intake even more. Our allowable water ration at this point was inadequate for our needs, even though we were still drinking about 3.5 quarts a day per person. If we managed to subsist on this ration, and climbed at this pace, we would need a half day more on the route than we'd planned and be just out of water as we finished. But it didn't work out that way.

On the 27th we pushed hard and reached the top of pitch 22, a hanging belay under a large roof. I was so dry now that my salivary glands had shut down, and I couldn't swallow without first adding water to my mouth. It took me an hour to eat a Clif Bar. Mark's dry heaves continued and his tongue got so physically stuck in his mouth that he had to push it around with his finger. We were feeling very weak and a little panicky, as conditions remained hot and windless. Even the nights had been hot; we slept with our sleeping bags barely covering ourselves. Mark went the day of the 27th without urinating, and I only urinated a small amount in the evening and early morning, none during the day.

The 28th was our sixth continuous day on the wall, and was to have been our summit day. We called a friend with our cell phone and asked him to meet us on top with water. We climbed pitch 23, the Dawn Roof, and stopped, completely exhausted, with four pitches to go and one quart per person left. The sun was relentless and the heat radiating off the rock felt like a sauna. We had found a little shady corner and I was thinking, "Should we go until we collapse?" Then I put my arm out in the sun and that did it! It was scorching. I thought, "I can't go out and lead this pitch."

We called the NPS rescue team at about noon and told them our situation. Water was all we needed and we didn't want to be hauled up. The rangers told us they would fly a team to the summit, lower a medic to us with several gallons of water, and make the decision then. We drank our last quart, and waited.

Our savior arrived about three hours later. He checked us over, decided we could continue, and left us on the route with four gallons, plus more that he would leave on top. We slept 12 hours that night after drinking our fill and finally eating a large meal. The next day was a different world. We were tired, with aches that mysteriously appeared for the first time as we re-hydrated, but the cotton-mouth was gone and we felt stronger. We topped out that evening having drunk about two gallons each in the preceding 24-hour period.

Analysis

Did we ask for a rescue because we had a cell phone and help was near? Maybe. But in our condition, either of us could have made a fatal mistake while climbing, or suffered heat stroke, with the same result. I'd been dry before and I thought I knew what dehydration was all about. We never doubted that we would be successful. It just had to get cooler, or maybe we would find water on a ledge higher up. But we were wrong, and we lost—we were truly cooked.

What to do as climbers? Accept that we run a razor's edge on dehydration. We rarely take enough water for our needs on big walls. Every big wall climber can attest to dark urine, infrequent urination, and thirst. That is the reality of climbing in the sunny world of Yosemite, but you still can't defeat the physiology, so take at least a conservative minimum. The average person loses about 2.5 quarts per day just sitting around, and the average athlete loses about one quart per hour during moderate exercise. So it's not surprising that we probably needed about five quarts per person per day to do the climb—dehydrated but functioning—in the conditions we experienced. That totals 15 gallons (125 pounds) for the two of us, in the haul bag.

What else would we do differently next time? Do not base plans on a weather forecast—plan for the worst, hope for the best. Bring an emergency stash beyond the carefully calculated rations, to compensate for dropped water, unforeseen delays, and unexpected weather. Substitute moist canned food, e.g., canned fruit, for some of the water, to keep caloric intake high. Minimize overly sweet water (Gatorade, etc.) or dilute it to avoid "sticky mouth." Keep the day's rations easily available and remind each other to drink. Start early each day and/or climb at night if conditions warrant, to reduce water loss. Bring a cheater stick to assist difficult retreats. We did not and decided it would be easier to continue up than to attempt a risky descent. (Source: Micha Miller and Mark Gunlogson)

(Editor's Note: It is always appreciated when those directly involved in an incident write such thorough reports. Oh, and for those of you who are not familiar with a "cheater stick," here's the word from John Dill: It's a short pole—3–4 feet long—with a carabiner (or other gadget) attached at the far end. You use it to clip protection that is out of your reach. If you're leading a hard aid pitch, you can "cheat" by reaching past a difficult placement. On an overhanging rappel, you can reach in to the wall, clip a bolt hanger or other fixed pro, and thereby stay close to the rock. Sticks used to be home-made (tent poles, etc.) but there is at least one commercial model now.)

FALL ON ICE–NO BELAY
California, Sierra Nevada, Mount Dana

On October 12, my wife, Ann (28) and I, Pedro Frigola (28), attempted a one-day ascent of Mount Dana via Dana Couloir, a popular 1,000-foot ice climb rated Class 4 ice/snow. Dana Couloir lies within the Ansel Adams Wilderness in the Sierra Nevada range and neighbors Yosemite National

Park on the other side of the peak. Ann and I have been climbing partners for six years and had previously attempted Mount Dana in June 2002, when we were turned back by high winds at the top of the couloir.

We set off at around 7 a.m. and reached Dana Glacier about three hours later. The weather was pleasantly calm with clear skies and light winds. The only other group on the mountain was a couple of climbers sorting gear at the base of the glacier. The glacier was free of snow, typical for this time of the year, and consisted of hard, lumpy ice and, in some places, hard water ice. The bergschrund, about one rope length above, was open. Further up, I could see the couloir gleaming with ice. We planned to simul-climb the length of the couloir, scramble to the summit and descend on the trail leading down to Tioga Pass. I racked the gear (including ice screws and quickdraws) and started a rising traverse towards the right side of the bergschrund. After most of the slack was out, Ann followed behind me. The glacier starts at a comfortable walking angle, then steepens to about 40 degrees near the bergschrund.

I remember climbing to within 20 feet of the bergschrund, stopping for a picture, and continuing to climb for another minute or so. I did not feel the need to place, and thus had not placed, any protection up to this point. I do not have any memory of the accident—whether it caught me by surprise, whether I tried to arrest the fall, the feeling of acceleration from sliding and tumbling for 200 feet—nothing. My next memory is that of crouching next to Ann, hearing the thumping of an approaching helicopter, and wondering why I was feeling so bad. Thus, Ann takes over the account of the next four hours, until shortly before my rescue.

Ann: While traversing the glacier, I tried to follow Pedro's path. However, shortly after we paused for a picture, I diverted slightly and came upon a patch of hard water ice. The angle of the glacier was still moderate, so I did not stop to find an alternate route or ask Pedro to place protection. As I took my next step, my foot slipped under me and I started to fall. My crampons did not hold my footing as I thought they would.

I instinctively yelled and tried to self arrest, but I could not dig my ice tool into the hard ice. I was sliding fast, expecting only the boulders at the base of the glacier to end my fall. All of a sudden, I stopped. I took a few seconds to gather my thoughts. As I was lying face down on the ice, I heard raspy, labored breathing emanating from a source nearby. It sounded like a bear, but it was Pedro. He had fallen to the same height as me, about 10 feet to the side. He lay upside down and a streak of blood originating from his face was trickling down the ice.

I had fallen approximately 100 feet and Pedro, who had started higher, close to 200 feet. While I had mostly slid down the glacier on my back and sides, Pedro had likely tumbled down when he was pulled off the ice by my fall. I called Pedro several times, but got no response. He was unconscious. I looked up and saw that our rope was caught on an ice outcropping, which had fortuitously stopped our fall. Level ground was still more than 150 feet below, so my first thought was to secure us in case the ice outcropping gave way. Pedro had all the ice screws. He was out of reach, but at this moment he regained consciousness. He tried standing up several times despite my urging him not to. He had lost an ice tool during the fall and was otherwise unable to place a screw, so I asked him to throw one to me. He fumbled for some time to unclip one, but once he did, to my surprise, he threw it to me accurately. I placed it and clipped myself in. Then I moved closer to Pedro, reached over and hooked his end of the rope with my ice tool. He'd moved enough that his full weight was no longer on the rope, so I was able to pull it to me and clip him to the same screw.

I could see that Pedro was disoriented, slow to respond and not fully coordinated. He appeared dazed and kept asking, "Why do I feel so bad?" There was blood all over his face, and he complained of a persisting, sharp pain in both wrists and the right knee.

Meanwhile, one of the two climbers we had seen earlier, who had witnessed our accident, climbed up to help. Paul, a mountain guide, was on a trip with his client, Kirill, who unwittingly got to experience mountain rescue firsthand. When Paul reached us, he asked Pedro some basic questions to assess his condition and Pedro accurately answered them all. I tried to summon help on the cell phone, but there was no reception. We knew it was necessary to get Pedro off the glacier on our own.

Paul set up an anchor and belayed Kirill up. Pedro was in no condition to downclimb or even to rappel himself, so Paul lowered him with Kirill, who supported him. Progress was slow as Pedro was reluctant to lean back on the rope. When the rope was almost out, Kirill set up an anchor and secured himself and Pedro. I then rappelled down and Paul down-climbed. We repeated the process once more until we reached a relatively flat area. We tried walking down the rest of the glacier with Kirill and Paul supporting Pedro, but in his dazed state, Pedro was hard to manage. So, we decided to stop there. Our first priority was to keep Pedro warm to prevent him from going into shock. Paul generously offered his ensolite pad, emergency blanket, and down vest and then hiked out to seek help. It was about noon. While we waited, Kirill made miso soup, but Pedro would only have warm water. He was still dazed and in pain and was beginning to shiver, as we were in the shade by now. I tried to keep him warm and awake and also bandaged his face, which had stopped bleeding. Time passed slowly. Finally, around 3 p.m., we heard the sound of a helicopter approaching. Pedro was stunned when I told him it was coming for him. He did not want to cause so much trouble. From this point on, Pedro recalls the events and resumes the account.

Pedro: The helicopter circled several times around the terminus of the glacier in search of a suitable landing spot and finally landed 100 yards away. A rescue crew of five quickly made their way to us and placed me in a full body splint and rescue litter. The helicopter hovered overhead, lowered a rope, and carried me (along with one rescuer) on a "short-haul" to a nearby ridge. I specifically recall how comfortable and warm I felt and the tremendous view of the glacier and surroundings. Once on the ridge, I was moved inside the helicopter and flown to the Tioga Road, where an ambulance was standing by to take me to Mammoth Hospital. Then the helicopter flew back to pick up Ann, who had a sprained ankle, and the rest of the crew. Ann got a ride to the hospital from a member of the Mono County Sheriff's Office.

After numerous X-rays and a CAT scan, the doctors at Mammoth Hospital informed me of the injuries: concussion, broken mandible, a badly broken left wrist, hairline fracture of the C5 vertebra, sprained knee, sprained clavicle and several lacerations to the face. The broken wrist turned out to be the worst. The fall had shattered my scaphoid, a notoriously difficult bone to heal, in five pieces, requiring surgery and three pins to put it back together. Five months after the accident, I am just beginning to regain motion in the joint. Still, things are progressing, and I hope to be back climbing come springtime.

Analysis

This is my first accident in nearly ten years of climbing. Although I consider myself a cautious climber, I must admit to having taken this climb for granted. I was focusing on the climb ahead and failed to appreciate the changing terrain. As the leader, I should have protected the climb using a running belay. In addition, I was carrying all the ice protection, leaving Ann ill-equipped to deal with the situation when I became injured. On future climbs, we will each carry appropriate gear.

Having time to reflect on the accident and the injuries I sustained, and more importantly the ones that I did not, I am very glad to have worn a helmet. There is no doubt my injuries would have been much more severe, if not fatal, had I not been wearing one. Although I felt no pain in my neck, I also turned out to have a hairline cervical fracture. Use of a cervical collar and backboard is standard procedure to prevent further spinal injury after such a trauma as mine. That gear is hard to come by on a glacier, but the result of improper movement in such a situation can be catastrophic. Whether to stay on the steep, cold ice, immobilized by a partner or descend to a safer, more comfortable environment is a tough call and a consideration every lay rescuer needs to think through. That is where Wilderness First Responder training can stack the cards in your favor. (Source: Pedro and Ann Frigola)

FALL ON ROCK, INADEQUATE PROTECTION/BELAY
California, Tahquitz Rock, The Step

On October 19, we believe that David Kellogg (32) and Kelly Tufo (41) had completed the climb and had finished up on Super Pooper or White Maiden's Walkway. They were taking down their belay system when one of them slipped, pulling both of them off. They fell about 700 feet to their deaths.

When found at the bottom of Tahquitz, the two were still roped together with the rope still in David's belay device. We also found David's cleaning tool broken in half. One half was next to David and the other half was about 30 feet away. Kelly's cleaning tool was still clipped to his harness.

Analysis

This is what we believe happened through analysis of the scene, interviews from witnesses, review of harnesses and gear at the county morgue, and re-examining the scene from top to bottom: We believe David had his cleaning tool out and was trying to retrieve the last cam when one of them slipped. Note that there are two possible exit routes that are safe to walk away from—if you don't slip or trip! The basic lesson: Stay on belay until you are in a position where there is no danger of a slip/trip that could pull you over the side. (Source: From a report submitted by Glenn Henderson, Riverside Mountain Rescue Unit)

FALL ON ROCK, CLIMBING ALONE AND UNROPED
California, Temple Crag, Venusian Blind Arête

Linnea Erickson (age 22) had told a friend that she planned to solo climb the Venusian Blind Arête route (IV, 5.7) on Temple Crag. On Friday, October 24 Linnea left her camp at Third Lake carrying a light pack containing climbing shoes, chalk bag, jacket, water, and food. She crossed the creek below Third Lake, followed the well-used use trail to the base of Temple Crag, successfully surmounted the permanent snowfield, and traversed below the Moon-Goddess Arête to the base of the intended route. She ascended the arête approximately 800 feet to the vicinity of a prominent gendarme. At this point she apparently fell into the gully between the Moon Goddess Arête and the Venusian Blind Arête. Her jacket was located directly beneath the prominent gendarme (about 200 feet) and her body was located on a ledge about 150 feet further down at about 11,500 feet elevation. She died instantaneously upon falling. She was reported missing on the morning of Sunday, October 26, and her body was spotted at 3:30 p.m. during a helicopter search. Her body was recovered Monday, October 27, by Inyo County Search & Rescue with the support of the USFS helicopter.

Analysis

Linnea had recently come west from New Hampshire. She had limited familiarity with the Sierra Nevada Mountains, having previously soloed Cathedral Peak (III, 5.7) in the prior week and Mount Sill and Mount Gayley the previous day. She was attempting a long and serious, albeit not technically difficult route. The nature of the routes on Temple Crag, however, tends to make route finding ability very important. It is easy to stray off the moderate climbing and onto difficult terrain. When her body was located, there was no indication of exactly where she fell or why. It is only possible to surmise that she may have been slightly off-route on more difficult climbing than the intended 5.7, or she may have encountered a loose rock (a common occurrence in the High Sierra). Free-solo ascents always carry the possibility of a fatal mistake, particularly in a setting where the climber has limited experience. (Source: Dave German, Inyo County Search & Rescue)

VARIOUS FALLS, OVERDUE, LOST, AND TWO MEDICAL EMERGENCIES
California, Mount Shasta

With above normal snowpack, climbing conditions remained fairly good through most of the season (May-September). This was the third year with no fatalities and decreasing rescues and searches. Helicopters were used only twice for the total of five rescues. A helicopter was used once during a search. Of the three searches, two involved climbing parties who ran later than expected and had to bivouac, while one involved a lost climber.

One contributing cause to this decrease in searches and rescues may be due to climbing safety education and information provided by the Mount Shasta Climbing Rangers through presentations in retail stores and outdoor clubs, contact with the public on the mountain, the web page and the telephone recording. In addition, information provided by the Station's front desk personnel has added to the public's safety.

Most of the public assists this season involved route finding, instruction on proper equipment use (glissading) and assistance with these skills. Commercial climbing guides performed two rescues and one search involving their clients. As far as search, rescue, and public assists go, it was a quiet season on Mount Shasta. (Source: Eric White–Climbing Ranger and Avalanche Specialist)

FALLING ROCK–DISLODGED
Colorado, Boulder Creek Canyon

On July 16, Emergency squads rescued a man who was pinned on the bank of Boulder Creek when a rock the size of a couch crushed his leg this morning. The man, identified as Boulder resident Douglas Shaw, writhed in agony for more than 30 minutes as crews used winches and chains to stabilize the rock and then inch it off Shaw's right leg. Shaw and two companions, identified as Mary Riddel and Simon Peck, were preparing to cross the creek on a traverse rope used to reach a climbing area on the southern slope of Boulder Canyon about ten miles west of Boulder. Riddel and Peck told rescuers that they were standing on the large rock around 9:45 a.m. while Shaw prepared to clip onto the traverse rope. The rock suddenly rolled and then slid onto Shaw's leg, crushing it. Freeing Shaw required closing CO Route 119 through Boulder Canyon for nearly an hour, causing traffic to back up more than a mile in each direction. Shaw remained conscious throughout the ordeal and was able to talk with rescue crews. He was taken by ambulance to Boulder Community Hospital at about 10:35 a.m. (Source: Greg Avery, Boulder Daily Camera, July 17, 2003)

FALL ON ROCK, PROTECTION CAME OUT
Colorado, Boulder Canyon, Cobb Rock

A 20-year-old Air Force Academy cadet fell about 65 feet while still attached to his line during a climb at Cobb Rock in Boulder Canyon on August 17. The initial report from a witness who called 911 about 3:20 p.m. was that the man, Martin K. Emerson (20), had fallen 65 feet and landed on his back. Rescuers found, though, that while climbing with fellow cadets, his grapples (sic) began coming loose in a "zipper fashion," and he was able to stay attached to his line and land feet first, the Sheriff's Office said. He then fell onto his back on a rocky ledge at the base of Cobb Rock. He was conscious but complaining of back pain after the impact, officials said. Members of the Rocky Mountain Rescue Group and Pridemark Paramedics traversed Boulder Creek and climbed to where Emerson was. He was given pain medication, carried across the creek and taken by ambulance to Boulder Community Hospital, where Sheriff's Office officials said he was in good condition. (From the *Boulder Daily Camera – Local Digest*, August 18, 2003)

(Editor's Note: We'll assume that "grapples" means protection. Surviving a 65-foot fall and ending up in good condition suggests a run of good luck.)

FALL ON ROCK–DISLODGED ROCK, WEATHER
Colorado, Snowmass Mountain

They'd waited a year to take another stab at summiting Snowmass Mountain after weather forced them to turn back last summer. On Saturday, two climbing buddies finally reached their goal, only to have their celebration end in tragedy.

A fluke accident coming down the mountain claimed the life of a 51-year-old Littleton hiker, who tumbled to his death as his horrified friend watched. Steve Castellano fell about 150 feet at 1:30 p.m. after he put his hand on a loose rock that was apparently teetering on soil softened by recent rain. "The rock gave way, which made him pitch forward," said Pitkin County Sheriff's Deputy Mario Strobl. "That caused him to fall head over heels." Castellano's friend, Bill Sudmeier of Denver, ran to the climber's aid. Sudmeier pressed a bandanna against a bleeding head wound and cradled his fellow climber in his arms while others in the area hiked out for help. Another passer-by attempted CPR, but Castellano died about a half-hour later. (From an article by Sarah Huntley, *Rocky Mountain News*, August 18, 2003)

Analysis

There have been a number of fatalities on Snowmass over the years, especially on the hiking routes, and often involving dislodged rocks. The sedimentary rock formation is an inherent peril, always made worse by rain. Source: Jed Williamson)

FALL ON ROCK, INADEQUATE PROTECTION, INEXPERIENCED
Colorado, Eldorado Canyon State Park, Calypso

On September 5, a climber (44) who was the third man on the rope started up the first pitch on Calypso when he fell, causing him to pendulum and thus hit the wall, resulting in breaking an ankle.

Analysis

The second climber had pulled all the protection as he went up. Because of the configuration of the route, the leader should have told the second to back-clip the protection. (Source: Steve Muelhauser, Park Manager II, Eldorado Canyon State Park)

(Editor's Note: Steve Muelhuaser indicated in an e-mail that this was the only reported accident of any significance in the park for 2003.)

FALLING ROCK–DISLODGED
Colorado, McCurdy State Park, Blockbuster

My partner was injured while climbing a route near "Blockbuster" on September 9. A loose block (about 6x6x4 feet) pulled while he was following. He struck his knee on the way down. Thankfully there was no compound fracture injury nor dire blood loss taking place, although the combination of lacerations, contusions, and weather (40 F) were conspiring to put him in to shock pretty quickly. (Source: Ryan Gamlin, posted on the climbing-boulder.com website, sent forward by Leo Paik)

(Editor's Note: Rocky Mountain National Park reported that there were no significant incidents to report from 2003. There are always a number of "overdues," but this year it appears there were no fatalities or serious injuries.)

FALLING ROCK, POOR POSITION
Montana, Beartooth Wilderness, Silver Run Peak

On August 24, around 0600, my wife, Rebecca Hodgkin, and I left camp —located just off the West Fork of Rock Creek Trail near Quinnebaugh Meadows—to climb Pensive Tower (III 5.8) on Silver Run Peak. At approximately 1100 we started the fifth pitch of the 9-10 pitch route. Rebecca was leading. Soon she was about thirty-five feet above me and out of sight. She took out a couple more feet of rope and declared, "I'm a little sketched out here!" There was a large loose boulder just laying in the granite seam above her. She said it was lying so precariously that if she did not knock it loose when she climbed above it, the rope surely would. I quickly evaluated my belay stance and determined, based on the small rocks clearing my head when I was standing erect and the fact that Rebecca had moved beyond an overhang, that hunkering down in a small alcove would undoubtedly be a good refuge from raining rocks. I assumed the position and called out, "Let her fly!"

From above I heard, "Here it comes!" I waited for the all too familiar clicking and clacking of falling rock but I heard nothing. Just as I was about to ask if she let it loose, the granite basketball hit me square in my back. The impact knocked me off the ledge and I swung like a pendulum due to my anchor being off to the side. In severe pain, I managed to get back on the ledge and lower Rebecca. She then put me on belay, and I down-climbed four feet to the left where there was a better ledge.

We are both Wilderness First Responders and took all of the necessary precautions for a spinal injury. We did a spine injury evaluation. I had proper motor function in both lower and upper extremities, as well as adequate sensation. I was alert and had no abnormal tingling sensation.

Upon palpation of the spine, however, I had ten or more vertebrae that were severely tender. It was clear that I needed to be fully immobilized and evacuated. In addition, I had severe pain in my right kidney area and I feared internal injuries. Rebecca gave me her jacket and she rappelled the route to initiate a rescue.

Around 1900, a helicopter, later identified to me as the Mammoth crew from Yellowstone National Park, made several passes but none near my area. I watched in desperation as they made an extensive search of the Castle and Medicine Mountain area, two to four miles away from my location. They searched our tent site area on the valley floor and what I believe to be the top of the ridge of Silver Run Peak. The closest they came was a single pass approximately 500 feet below me. I waved a red jacket in vain, and around 2000 they disappeared southeast near Mount Lockhart. As the night went on, I fluctuated from mild to severe hypothermia. I shivered uncontrollably, and when the shivering disappeared I ate something to make it come back.

Around 0500, my friend, Thaddeus Josephson, and Rebecca reached me with warm clothes and a down sleeping bag. They had no communications with the official rescue party so Thaddeus rappelled the route to meet them at the bottom of the climb. Rebecca stayed on the ledge with me. At 0900, two rescuers from the Grand Teton National Park, Scott and Dave, got short hauled to my ledge. They secured me to a backboard and short hauled me to the valley floor. Rebecca was also taken off the ledge via the short haul. I was then flown to Red Lodge where a connecting helicopter took me to Billings Hospital. My diagnosis: several bruised vertebrae in the thoracic and lumbar area, one of which had a compressed disc and was possibly fractured. I also had a fracture in a floating rib and a severely bruised kidney.

Analysis

Was it a poor decision to let the rock loose? We had several other options: First, we could have backed off the climb. We would have had to leave gear and risk more rock fall by pulling ropes over very loose terrain. Second, we could have chosen a different line. The rock, however, was blank granite and would have been unprotected and almost certainly above our climbing abilities. Third, I could have moved my belay stance. Knowing now the rock's trajectory, this probably would have been the best option. Over the years of climbing I, like most climbers I believe, have a short-term memory when it comes to potentially fatal near misses. I had grown too accustomed to having rocks whiz by at high speed and never fully registered their danger.

Why did the first rescue helicopter never find me? Rebecca gave a detailed description of my location using a topographic map. The Sheriff's department translated Rebecca's description to numbers using a computer program and came up with a position nearly two miles away. GPS units are cheap and should be considered on remote trips. (Source: Mr. Hodgkin)

FALL ON ROCK—RAPPEL ERROR, NO BELAY OR BACK-UP, INEXPERIENCE
North Carolina, Pilot Mountain State Park

On March 15, Russell Page (22) was participating in a rappel training exercise near one of the access gullies, west of the Amphitheater. He was with a group of EMS/Firefighters from Forsyth Community College (NC) when he fell to the ground below.

The instructor, Mike Maher, also a witness to the accident stated that the group of ten students had just completed the instructional section of their training when Russell was beginning to rappel. According to Maher, Russell "panicked" as he went over the cliff edge, lost control, and fell approximately 40 feet to the rocks below, landing head-first.

Two members of the group went to the parking lot, a short distance away to call 911. Since most of the participants in the group were EMTs or Paramedics, first aid was started immediately. Russell was semi-conscious throughout the incident and was described as "combative" by rescue personnel. Even though he was wearing a helmet, the length of the fall combined with his body weight of 240 pounds caused his helmet to collapse, resulting in a severe skull fracture.

He was evacuated by Pilot Knob Rescue through a high angle rescue and transported via helicopter to Wake Forest Medical Center in Winston Salem, NC. He is expected to recover.

Analysis

According to the Park Superintendent who was on the scene, Russell was not belayed. When the instructors were asked about this, their reply was that they didn't use one because Russell had rappelled before, and that they were not using any back-up systems for any students.

It is standard practice for individuals participating in any organized or sponsored climbing and/or rappelling activity be belayed, either by a separate belay rope (by a prusik loop attached to the climbers leg harness loop), or at the least using a "fireman's belay." Being surrounded by a group of EMTs and Paramedics and wearing a helmet may have been the contributing factors that saved Russell's life. (Source: Andy Whitaker, Pilot Mountain State Park and Aram Attarian)

AVALANCHE
New Hampshire, Canon Mountain, Black Dike

Two climbers were up to attempt the Black Dike in the beginning of April. They weren't really thinking about the possibility of an avalanche. It's not clear how often anyone thinks of that small gully sliding. In retrospect all the ingredients were there. Perfect slope angle, heavily wind loaded lee slope, and lots of fresh faceted powder. TP always tried to hug the wall a little bit near the Whitney-Gilman (left), just in case, and he was a bit near it this day, just not enough evidently. For some reason when they cleared the trees and got about fifty feet from the rescue cache, TP took off his pack and put on his helmet. There was a lot of unfamiliar ice up on the cliffs from the recent freezing rain and it made him a little uncomfortable, so he put the helmet on early, an action he gave true thanks for after he cracked it on the slide.

They started post-holing up that gully. About ten feet into it, TP hit the "sweet spot" and set off the whole thing. He estimated the crown was about 12-18 inches deep and approximately 50 feet wide. As soon as it fractured, they were gone. TP tried to run towards the cliff but was immediately overrun and sent head-first down into the talus. By the time he stopped he had slid somewhere between 50-100 feet. His partner slid approximately 200 feet. He quickly realized that he was OK, experiencing just some serious bruising. He found his partner after he was able to clear his throat and mouth of snow and was able to access his situation, he claimed to be OK, but really "beat up."

As TP put it "we just both put our heads down and marched, slid, crawled and groaned our way back to the truck, an event which you can probably recreate in your imagination." They went to the hospital where DR was diagnosed with with three fractured vertebrae and a bruised kidney, among other assorted ailments not as serious. TP didn't go to the hospital. It took him about a week to recover to 100 percent.

Analysis
Awareness is everything. Many people don't perceive this area as a possible avalanche slope, but it has done so in the past. It almost got alpinist John Bouchard, and several years previously Jared Ogden was caught in one in the same area and injured his back. On this day the conditions were right for the slope to let go, and it did.

If the climbers had been pinned or buried, it might have been a day or two before anyone realized what had taken place, due to the time of year and lack of climbing traffic. Canon is a true alpine environment and should be treated with respect. (Source: Al Hospers)

FALL ON ROCK, INADEQUATE PROTECTION
New Hampshire, Saco Crag, Roadside Attraction
On Saturday, May 31, a first-season leader and his partner were starting up Roadside Attraction, 5.9+ on Saco Crag, north of Cathedral Ledge. The leader used a nut as his first piece to protect the opening crux moves and had fallen onto the gear several times. The belayer was securely anchored to a large tree at the base of the route, situated over a steep and exposed slab that drops off to the base of the cliff. A nearby climber saw the falls and advised the leader that his nut placement had shifted and he should put in a multi-directional cam to protect the crux. The leader was satisfied with the gear he had and made another attempt to climb, but this time his fall pulled the nut out. Apparently he fell onto his back and slid approximately 15 feet down the slab, where his belayer caught him. His belayer or a bystander tied off the lead rope to the tree using an overhand (non-releasable) knot.

A local guide and friend arrived at the cliff to find one EMT and one climber on the slab holding a backboard under the victim. The assisting climber was tied onto a tree above, but the EMT was not. They could not lower the victim to the board due to the fixed knot on the weighted lead rope, and they could not set the board securely under the victim. At this point, the victim was complaining of considerable pain from hanging in his harness. The guide lowered a free end of the rope for them to tie to the victim's belay loop and secured it to an anchor on the tree using a Munter hitch. Once the victim was lifted several inches, enough to release the fixed knot, they were able to lower him onto the backboard. For carry out, the victim was secured to the backboard, and Mark set an anchor on a tree above the steep trail down to the road. The guide fixed a rope to the backboard and belayed them down the trail using a Munter knot on the tree. The victim was met by a waiting ambulance, was transported to Memorial Hospital, and released later that day, since his injuries were apparently fairly minor.

Analysis

The leader later acknowledged that he had so far lead nothing harder than 5.7 prior to trying Roadside Attraction!

Tying the victim to the tree with a fixed knot rather than a releasable knot caused much of the confusion on the scene. It is unclear to me why Mountain Rescue Service was not called for this accident, considering the high angle and technical complexity. Had Mark and I not happened upon the scene, it could have taken much longer. (Source: Al Hospers)

FALL ON ROCK, INADEQUATE PROTECTION
New Hampshire, Cathedral Ledge, Recompense

In October, on the third pitch of Recompense, my partner, Mark, was ten feet from topping out and went to plug a cam and popped off. He was 15 feet above his last piece, so with rope stretch fell about 35 feet and hit the small ledge about 15 feet above the belay stance. It was immediately apparent that his arm/wrist was badly injured, but all other digits intact. No head injury and he was coherent. We lowered him down (shouting the whole way that a 911 call wasn't necessary, but those who saw his fall were pretty freaked out).

I lowered off and we walked out, then drove to the ER. He broke his wrist in three places and dislocated the bones in his palm. He spent two hours in surgery getting pins put in.

Analysis

It was totally obvious that his pride was hurt more than anything. He's an experienced climber and has led Recompense four times and never fallen. This goes to show that just because you have a climb wired doesn't mean you should run it out 15 feet when there's good pro. We were lucky that it was just a broken wrist.

I was very impressed with our climbing community that day. Everyone on and around the prow came quickly to our aid and organized a clean descent. Anyway, that's the scoop. (Source: From an e-mail to Al Hospers from Holly.)

(Editor's Note: There were a few other reports from NH, but none involving serious injury. Two of them were simply stranded climbers.)

VARIOUS FALLS ON ROCK (17), RAPPEL ERRORS (5), INADEQUATE BELAYS (5), INADEQUATE PROTECTION (5), PROTECTION PULLED (2), DISLODGED ROCKS (2)
New York, Shawangunks

There were 24 accidents reported from the Shawangunks this year, of which 18 happened while ascending. There was one fatality, occurring in March when an experienced 44 year-old climber fell while leading Strictly from Nowhere (5.7). He did not protect the traversing moves out to the end of the overhang. His fall was backwards—about ten or twelve feet—and he struck his head. He was not wearing a helmet.

There were five rappelling incidents, three of which were the result of going off the end of the rope. One involved four climbers, because when the rappel rope jammed, several rocks were dislodged in trying to free up the rope. The average age of the climbers directly involved was 33, the youngest being 16, the oldest being 51. Most of the routes were of modest difficulty. One accident involved Mike Cimino (32), a guide, who fell while leading Transcontinental Nailway, a 5.10 route. A piece of protection pulled, so he fell 20 feet to the ground on his back, resulting in "...six fused vertebrae, a couple of broken ribs, and a renewed sense of enthusiasm." His own analysis, for which we thank him, is as follows:

"Hubris got me hurt. I've climbed the route lord knows how many times... I was working a 'rope-gun' day (meaning nothing but single pitch 5.10 and 5.11 lines) with one of my regulars. ...I made poor decisions: no helmet (thankfully not a major factor) and I chose a tiny blue alien rather than a larger yellow one with a nut back-up as my first piece. When the unlikely fall happened, my gear was simply inadequate. As a guide, it's all too easy to slip into thinking of the gear as only being there as directionals for the clients' protection."

The Mohonk Preserve Ranger Team comprised of seven individuals has now completed about 500 rescues. They are trained in pre-hospital care and engage in weekly drills. Their ability to respond to a range of accident types has resulted in reducing morbidity and fatality, and in being asked to train military, police, and other rescue personnel. (Sources: Hank Alicandri –Director of Land Stewardship/Head Ranger, and Mike Cimino.)

STRANDED, WEATHER, INADEQUATE EQUIPMENT–NO STOVE
Oregon, Mount Hood, Reid Glacier Headwall

This incident involved a climbing team that was part of a Portland-area climbing club. The following description of the events leading to the incident on January 11 and 12 was derived from an explanation provided by the climbing team.

Our intent was to climb the Leuthold Couloir. When we started up the Palmer Snowfield there were a couple of mild snow flurries and it was partly cloudy at Illumination Saddle. The weather cleared and was great as we traversed over to the start of the Leuthold climb. Around 9,800 feet we mistakenly took a gully to the right of the Leuthold Couloir that put us on the Reid Headwall. The weather conditions were still good at this time.

Although I did not record times as to where we were, we seemed to be making good progress during this part of the climb. Once inside the gully on Reid Headwall poor snow conditions slowed climbing. We ran into loose, sugary snow conditions in steep areas that required belays.

As we made our way up through the more technical sections of the headwall, the weather started to deteriorate and we were hampered by poor visibility. I was becoming increasingly concerned about time but down-climbing the Reid Glacier Headwall would have placed us in danger on several known avalanche-prone slopes. Up and over was determined to be the safest route as many in the team were familiar with this part of the mountain.

As we traversed along the top of Reid Headwall towards the summit ridge, the storm had picked up strength. Strong winds and marble-sized hail hampered visibility that was poor anyway as it was starting to get dark.

We continued toward the summit with the hope of reaching the Pearly Gates before it got totally dark. We felt confident we could navigate down from there with our headlamps.

When down-climbing safely became increasingly difficult due to the poor visibility, we regrouped and had one party member climb down to make sure we were on route. He ran into a short vertical rock band and came back up. By this time party members were getting cold, so we decided to dig in and descend in the morning.

There were two reasons we called 911. (1) To inform the authorities that we were overdue and safe in a snow cave 80 meters below the summit. (2) Two party members were trending towards hypothermia and notification was given to the authorities in case assistance would be required to bring the climbers down if their conditions worsened.

The following morning two teams of rescuers ascended the mountain to search for the climbers. Winds averaged around 30-40 mph with heavy snow and twenty feet of visibility compounded efforts to reach the climbers.

Analysis

One lesson from this accident is that no matter how experienced or prepared you are, the weather in the mountains (particularly the Cascades of Oregon and Washington) can change very rapidly and storms may arrive sooner and harder than expected.

Climbers should consider all possibilities when preparing for a climb and plan their strategy so they can avoid storms, and survive them. Frequently this is a balance between going lightweight to avoid moving slowly on dangerous terrain, but not going so lightweight that you are unable to survive if you become stranded. In this case, these climbers acted properly once they realized they were in trouble. They had adequate equipment and knowledge to survive. Rather than wandering around in a whiteout and risking becoming more seriously injured or disoriented, they protected themselves from the elements and called for help when they were unsure they would be able to self-rescue.

The leader of the climb made the following points:

• There had been forecasts of weather turning bad late in the day. Doing this climb with a fairly large party and uncertain weather and nothing more than emergency bivy gear left a smaller margin of safety.

• Route finding: Although I had climbed Leuthold before I did not remember the spot where we went to the right. Had I been paying proper attention I should have figured it out soon enough to get back on Leuthold and we would have made the summit before dark.

• Leadership: When the party started going slowly I should have taken control more. One option would have been to shorten the rope so I could communicate with the team better.

• Poor equipment planning: In hindsight, I can't believe that I had not included a stove in our equipment. Our near hypothermia could have been avoided. Also, the frostbite, from which one other team member and I have fully recovered, could have been avoided.

• Communication: When we originally called 911, we stated our intent to descend in the morning if the condition of the team did not deteriorate any further. We were advised to stay where we were and that a team would be mobilized to ascend. One other team member and myself were borderline hypothermic early in the evening but our condition improved in the snow cave. Although we communicated to the people at the rescue base that we were all ambulatory but cold, we should have been more assertive in holding to our decision to descend on our own in the morning. In our attempt to be agreeable with the SAR effort we needlessly endangered several of the rescuers.

A final note from Steve Rollins: Avalanche danger rose quickly during this storm, threatening to prevent rescuers from being able to reach the stranded party safely. Had conditions been any worse, it is possible rescue efforts would have been postponed, resulting in the party being stranded for an even longer period of time. Climbers should be aware that rescuer safety always takes precedence and therefore rescues are not always possible. (Sources: Steve Rollins–Portland Mountain Rescue; David Byrne–35; Jim Brewer–48; Bob Pelletie–38; Jared Cogswell–31; Keith Campbell–44; and a story from *The Oregonian*.)

FALL ON ROCK–CLIMBER LOWERED OFF END OF ROPE BY BELAYER
Oregon, Smith Rock State Park, Magic Light

On February 21, Timothy Garland (24) climbed Magic Light in the Overboard Area of Smith Rock State Park. Magic Light is a bolted route rated 5.12b, two stars by Alan Watts in his Climber's Guide to Smith Rock. The lower portion is rated 5.11a and is often climbed, but the upper portion contains the real difficulties and is less frequently climbed according to Watts.

Tim easily reached the top anchors and was lowered off. He knew the rope was short and expected to be stopped to reset the top rope. Instead, he was lowered off the end of the top rope belay, falling a reported 75 to 100 feet sustaining a broken back, ribs, and sternum and internal injuries according to Oregon State Park records. He was air-lifted to St. Charles Hospital in Bend.

Analysis

Four months before this top rope failure, a similar serious incident had occurred at Smith Rock: The belayer dropped the top roped climber about 30 feet off the end of the rope. Typically, the belayer is concentrating on the climber being lowered, failing to mind the remaining belay rope. Sport climbers typically do not tie into the bottom end of the top belay rope. Tying a stopper knot or tying the rope into the sport rope bag would have prevented these incidents. Smith Rock Ranger David Slaight says he now reminds climbers to always tie a simple knot near the end of the belay rope.

Timothy Garland is a well liked 5.13 climber according to Redpoint Guide Jim Ablao, and is pictured in a popular climbing desk calendar. He is back climbing again, although the belayer, whose name was not released, has not climbed at Smith since the incident. (Source: Robert Speik)

FALL ON ROCK, PARTY SEPARATED
Oregon, North Sister

Dr. Bruce Shively (55) slipped on the steep friable volcanic rock slopes below the summit of North Sister and fell 600 vertical feet to his death, down one of three possible chutes. Shively was last seen about 2:30 p.m. on Saturday while descending the dangerous unstable slopes. He became separated from his female climbing partner who did not see him fall. She descended and two hours later borrowed a cell phone to call for Search and Rescue. At 4:30 pm. on Sunday, Dr. Shively's body was observed closely from an Oregon National Guard helicopter by Al Hornish, a mission manager with Deschutes County Search and Rescue. It was determined Shively had not survived the fall.

Dr. Shively's body was recovered by helicopter hoist on July 11, by Lane County Search and Rescue Personnel according to John Miller, SAR Coordinator.

Analysis

North Sister is a fourth-class climb to the summit, approached along the top of the south ridge by a faint climber's way high up along the west side of a gendarme called The Camel's Hump. The route then winds to the east side of a second gendarme, then traverses across an exposed friable 35 degree slope just under the Prouty Pinnacles to a gully called The Bowling Alley. Most groups, equipped with helmets and rock climbing skills, will elect to set a hand-line across this traverse and belay and rappel the loose gully to the summit.

Five climbers have died in recent years on North Sister, some from inexperience and a failure to mitigate the high exposure and objective dangers of this old volcano.

Dr. Shively was reportedly an experienced climber, having summited Mount Hood, Mount Adams, and Mount St. Helens. However, climbing these moderate snow clad peaks is not adequate preparation for the steep friable volcanic slopes guarding the gendarmes and summit blocks of North Sister. (Source: Robert Speik)

FALL ON ROCK, PARTY SEPARATED
Oregon, Middle Sister

On August 15, Trent Gabel (16) fell to his death, most likely from dislodging rocks, while attempting to climb a route on Middle Sister. He was with Pathfinders Youth Group from Tillamook, and at the time of his fall was accompanied by an adult. But they became separated when Gabel moved out of sight to check out the route ahead while his partner was taking photographs. (Source: Jeff Scheetz, John Miller, and two articles from *The Oregonian*.)

FALLING ROCKS
Utah, Big Cottonwood Canyon, Storm Mountain

On February 17th, Kris (27) was hit by spontaneous rockfall while practicing solo aid-climbing on Six-appeal, a 5.6 bolted route at the Storm Mountain picnic area in Big Cottonwood Canyon. The bolts are spaced widely on this route, and he was placing small nuts between them. The rope was anchored at the bottom end, and he was using a clove-hitch as his solo-device, backed up by a figure-eight knot further along the rope.

He was also moving a fixed line up the route as he climbed, fixing it to the top bolt each time he passed one. Temperatures were warm for February and snowmelt was running down the route and down a chimney left of the route. Kris had moved up and down parts of the route several times when a rock slab released spontaneously from the chimney. He estimated the size of the rock to be ten feet by three feet by one foot thick. He jumped away from the rock and managed to avoid most of the contact. The slab hit his foot on the way by, breaking his ankle, tibia, and fibula in five places. Smaller rocks also hit his face and helmet. He took about an eight-foot fall, ending up hanging from a bolt secured by the clove-hitch. He was able to switch to his fixed line and rappel to the bottom of the route. Climbers from the nearby Bumblebee Wall had heard the rockfall and knowing that Kris was on the route, they came by to check on him and called for help. SAR members met them at the base of the crag and carried Kris to the road where he was transported by ground ambulance. He spent three months in bed or on crutches and has now recovered and plans to climb again this summer.

Analysis

Kris was an experienced climber, wearing a helmet, and practicing good techniques on an easy route. Solo aid climbing can sometimes produce huge fall-forces compared to normal lead falls, but all of his gear held. Spontaneous rockfall can happen at any time, but it is by far the most likely in Spring freeze-thaw cycles, when cracks are forced wider by snow and ice, and then the ice melts, taking out the "glue" holding the rocks together. This is a spot that gets climbed thousands of times a year, and appears solid. It's not known for rockfall, though perhaps it should be. I've personally had my closest call from rockfall about ten feet away from this, just on the other side of the chimney. (Source: Tom Moyer–Salt Lake County Sheriff's Search and Rescue)

FALL ON SNOW–UNABLE TO SELF-ARREST DURING VOLUNTARY GLISSADE, POOR POSITION, WEATHER
Washington, Mount Rainier National Park, Mount Ruth

On June 22, a group of nine Mountaineers and I set off to attempt Mount Ruth, a spur-peak on the north-east flank of Mount Rainier. As we encountered snow several hundred feet below Glacier Basin, the starting point of our ascent, Mount Ruth would be classified as a "snow scramble."

Around 1:00 p.m., we achieved the summit without incident. After soaking up the sun rays filtering through the rapidly moving clouds, we began our descent. After descending less than 1000 feet, the clouds thickened and engulfed us. An occasional fleeting sunny break allowed us to find our route. Leadership with respect to route finding on the descent was rather informal and the group diverged as we descended. As realized only later, several of us ended up considerably to the left of the relatively slope we had ascended. Our descent trajectory placed us directly above the rock cliff bands purposely avoided during our ascent.

The urge to glissade in the mushy summer snow was irresistible to many of us, although a few individuals refrained, perhaps more cautious as a result of greater experience with the conditions confronting us that day. Although I had never been an overly enthusiastic "glissader," I became caught up in the excitement of the moment and followed several others. In proper glissade position (as taught by the Seattle Mountaineers), I found myself "racing" a fellow Mountaineer when the clouds once again descended upon us. Immediately, I forced my ice ax into the snow to act as a brake. With no immediate reduction in velocity and continued acceleration, I instinctively rolled over into a perfect textbook self-arrest position. To my shock and disbelief, my acceleration continued.

Earliest memories of the initiation of my fall are of sheer terror. I vaguely recalled the series of rock bands, and that they protruded perhaps 20 feet above the height of the snow. Realizing I was well above them, logic continued in my thoughts, and as seconds passed, I speculated that if I hit the rock band, my fall would terminate.

I was not stopped by the rock band. It acted more as a springboard, deflecting my fall over its rocky edge. I was then thrown through a long narrow rock chute approximately 300 feet in height, extending from the top of the cliff band to an open snow field littered with various sized rock debris from the cliffs above. I was ejected onto a snowfield of lesser slope scattered with boulders and situated at a drastically lower elevation. My final resting position was within 500 vertical feet of the floor of Glacier Basin. I found myself in a sitting position amidst a field of rock debris. An unforgettable intense emotional outburst ensued.

I was wearing a high-tech tee shirt, Goretex rain-pants and a day pack, all of which were still attached. My vision was blurry. My prescription sunglasses were gone. Some time elapsed before I realized I could move my head. I could not feel my arms and I had severe pain in both legs. Looking down, I saw blood running down my left arm. There was blood over my shredded rain pants. I attempted to move my right arm and found I was able to. I grabbed my left arm with my right arm and attempted to maneuver the left arm to better evaluate the extent of the injuries. I repeated the exercise on my legs. Nothing appeared to be broken.

Injuries included multiple puncture wounds, cuts, scrapes and bruises to both arms, a deep puncture wound to the right shin, heavy bruising on right quadriceps and other regions of both legs. Nerve damage in the left elbow resulted in lack of sensation in the fingers and limited mobility of the left arm for two months. I recall my head hitting against rock on several occasions; however, there were no visible marks from these impacts, and I never lost consciousness, even though I was not wearing a helmet. I believe my well-stuffed backpack prevented more serious injuries. I suffered some memory loss of part of the fall.

Coincidentally, I had taken a photo of the rock bands located between Glacier Basin and Mount Ruth during our ascent, although we had not ascended by this route due to the steepness. When compared to the topographical map of the region, the photos and map together provided the capability to measure the extent of my fall. Using Green Trails map number 270, Mount Rainier East, I calculated the total elevation loss during my fall to be about 1600 feet. The rock cliff I plummeted over was approximately 300 feet in height.

Looking back up at the mountain, I could not see any members of my party. Although it was painful, I attempted to stand-up with my intent being to plunge-step the remaining 500 feet to the floor of the basin and safety. I appeared to be in rock fall zone at the base of the rock chute. I staggered down the slope, using my ice ax as a cane. After what seemed an eternity of stumbling downhill, I arrived at my destination, a large relatively flat pile of gravel-sized rock. While starting to attend to my injuries, I gazed up at the mountain and saw small "dots." I instinctively recognized as my fellow Mountaineers. I waved my ice ax, hoping I would be spotted. Fortunately, one member from my party was well ahead of the others and reached me about an hour and a half after my fall. He assessed my injuries and provided first aid.

Analysis

Key factors attributing to this event were over-confidence in ability of ice ax to self-arrest, glissading under unsuitable conditions, and not knowing the descent route. All these were exacerbated by poor weather. The lessons I learned were that the effectiveness of ice ax in self-arrest technique is variable to the point of complete failure and that glissading should not be practiced during unsuitable conditions. (Source: Tim Nair)

FALL ON ROCK, FATIGUE, INADEQUATE PROTECTION
Washington, Cascades, Chimney Rock

On July 6, on the sixth pitch of the East Face of Chimney Rock, Ralph Leach (50) was leading. He was showing signs of fatigue after moving about 20 feet. He had two pieces of pro in. After trying for a while two get a third piece in at about 30 feet, he decided to move on up, looking for a better placement for the pro. This is when he peeled off and fell 30 feet. The rope caught him just short of hitting the deck. But 15 feet into the fall, he hit a blocky ledge, seriously injuring both feet. (Fractured left heel and an open dislocation of the right ankle.)

Given that there were just the two climbers on the mountain and no one else available to assist, evacuation was going to be a slow process requiring extreme vigilance. After lowering the injured climber using his belay device, his partner Rod Xuerb (47) would retrieve the rope and rappel to the new position. After repeating this procedure a few times, a ledge suitable for a bivouac was reached at 7,000 feet. After securing the injured climber at 6:00 p.m., Rod continued to descend and go out for help. After only eighteen hours a National Guard helicopter performed the evacuation the following morning.

Analysis

A willingness to back off on days that you are not up to the demands of the climb could prevent an accident such as this. Rod had offered to lead the pitch, but Ralph thought that he was up to it at the outset. The level of skill at placing protection may have been a factor. (Source: Ralph Leach and Rod Xuerb.)

(Editor's Note: These two climbers provided a lengthier description that included details about the lower/descent. We appreciate their willingness to contribute.)

FALL ON ROCK–RAPPEL ERROR (NO BACK-UP), AND DISLODGED ROCKS
Washington, Snow Creek Wall, Outer Space

On September 22, William Tharpe (28) died in a rappelling accident on Snow Creek Wall near Leavenworth, Washington. Tharpe and his partner, M (27), were climbing Outer Space, a popular, six pitch, 5.9 route. M led the route's crux 5.9 pitch above Two Tree Ledge. Tharpe then started leading the more moderate pitch that ends on a feature known as "The Pedestal." There was now a party of two on the route below them. Tharpe placed several pieces of protection in the dihedral on the right side of The Pedestal, including a #3 Camalot near the top. He fell approximately fifteen feet onto the Camalot.

He and M could not see one another, but were able to yell back and forth. Tharpe said he had injured his left arm, shoulder, and ribs and asked to be lowered to the belay. He was told there was not enough rope, so he asked to be lowered as far as possible to where he could still construct an anchor, and then rappel the remaining distance to M. That location turned out to be about 20 feet above and 20 feet left of M. M could see Tharpe's upper body, but he could not see the anchor and the rope through it, nor could he see the ends of the rope.

Tharpe fell within a short distance of starting the rappel, pulling the rope with him. He hit Two-Tree Ledge, then continued to fall to the base of the wall. Rock was somehow dislodged in the fall, and the lead climber on the pitch below was struck on the head but not incapacitated. The second party regrouped on Two-Tree Ledge, where they were able to communicate with M and made a cell phone call for assistance.

Tharpe was dead when Chelan County Mountain Rescue volunteers reached the scene. The Chelan County Coroner's report stated he died of "multiple internal injuries due to blunt impact to the head and chest." His belay/rappel device (a Black Diamond ATC) had only one bight of rope threaded through it and clipped to the carabiner on his harness. One end of the rope extended an estimated 20 to 30 feet from the ATC. The long end was wrapped around his torso and stretched out of the lower Wall. The ends of the rope were not tied together, nor were there any knots in the individual ends of the rope. The rope had a middle marker. There was no gear on the rope. A runner from his harness tie-in loop was clipped to a gear loop. It probably had been used to connect to the rappel anchor. Tharpe was not wearing a helmet, but a helmet probably would not have prevented his death from the estimated 350 to 400 foot fall.

The other party of two descended from the climb on their own. A USFS fire fighting crew, assisted by Sheriff's Office deputies and CCMR, transported Tharpe's body to the trailhead. CCMR volunteers assisted M to the top of the wall. He recovered the gear left by Tharpe as he ascended. The rappel anchor consisted of two Aliens equalized with a long runner, backed up with an unequalized nut. There was a locking carabiner on the runner, presumably for connecting the rappel rope to the anchor.

Analysis

We can only hypothesize about the cause of the accident since M was not in a position to observe it. From M's inspection of the rappel anchor it appears there was no anchor failure. The 20 to 30 feet of rope extending from one side of the rappel device suggests Tharpe probably forgot to equalize the rope to its center and rappelled ten to 15 feet off the short end. Another possible explanation is that only one bight through the ATC was properly clipped and that Tharpe lost control of the ropes once the system was weighted. Tharpe would have also had to forget to equalize the two sides of the rope, or he could have consciously decided to pull through the anchor what he thought was just enough rope to make the short rappel to M's position. Thirty feet might have made it, but 20 feet probably would not have. Other explanations of how the short end resulted are possible. The extent of any injuries incurred in the original fall are unknown, but they could have caused him to alter his normal procedure for rappel setup or been a source of distraction.

What we do know is that Tharpe did not employ any backup mechanism that might have saved his life. The two primary methods of backup for preventing some mistakes or loss of control in a rappel do have drawbacks to be aware of, and some climbers choose not to use them. One backup commonly used is to knot the ends of the rope to prevent them from being pulled through the braking hand and/or an ATC-style of braking device. Tying both ends together is safer than tying a separate knot in each end. If just one bight through a rappel device gets clipped and loss of rope control occurs, a knot in a single end can pull through a rappel anchor, even one as small as a rappel ring if the knot is small. Also, if one uses a rappel device, such as a figure-eight, with large rope passageways, a larger knot is less likely to be pulled through the device.

The other backup is the use of a prusik or other friction knot on the rappel ropes and connected to the climber's harness. It is normally meant for stopping a runaway rappel if the climber loses control of the braking, or for a deliberate stop in the rappel, freeing the hands for other use. One might react quickly enough to lock a prusik knot used above the rappel device after an unknotted end passed through ones braking hand, but a prusik or autoblock knot applied below the rappel device would not have been of any use in this instance.

We are again reminded that there are many details to pay attention to in rappelling, and therefore much potential for error. The self-check procedure should include a look for the middle marker of the rope at the anchor point and a look at the rope below. Before unclipping from the anchor, test-weight the rappel and then check the orientation of your locking carabiner, what it is clipped to, and that the gate is closed and locked. Assess the consequences of not using a backup mechanism. (Source: Freeman Keller and Fred Stanley)

VARIOUS INCIDENTS AND SOME DATA
Washington, Mount Rainier National Park, Mount Rainier
There were 9,714 climbers registered in 2003, a relatively light year when compared to the record high of 13,114 in 2000. Of those registered, 3,520 were led by a guide service and the remainder climbed independently. Disappointment Cleaver remains Mount Rainier's most popular route. Over 4,700 climbers registered for it this year.

Camp Muir and Camp Schurman were staffed almost daily throughout June, July, and August. Climbing rangers provided updated route, weather, and safety information. Toilets were regularly cleaned and maintained. For example, the door to the Camp Schurman toilet had to be replaced twice because of wind damage.

Climbing rangers staffed the Paradise and White River Ranger Stations for more than 1,200 hours. Climbing-specific information and general public service is provided at these locations daily from Memorial Day to Labor Day, with weekend coverage in May and September.

High altitude, expansive glaciers, pristine beauty, and easy access make Mount Rainier one of North America's most popular mountaineering destinations. To ensure its preservation, the National Park Service works closely with climbers to eliminate additional impacts in fragile alpine areas. Some important tenets of resource protection include properly disposing of human waste, never creating new rock walls or tent platforms, staying on trails, and packing out all trash. In 2003, over 35 barrels of human waste (six tons) were collected from high camps and Panorama Point. However, rangers also noted over 170 incidents of improper human waste disposal around the mountain. Rangers carried down over 650 pounds of trash from high camps, collapsed 213 cairns, dismantled 81 rock walls, and contacted 23 parties who were camping in high impact zones. But the majority of climbers do their part and "leave no trace," allowing climbing rangers to spend most of their time and energy working directly with the public.

This year there were eight major rescues and no fatalities. Along the way, climbing rangers responded to a variety of other incidents such as: 19 medicals, 127 climber assists, five litter carryouts, and ten "mini" searches.

Some of the major and more interesting rescues of 2003 included:

Assistance to nine hypothermic and disoriented climbers on the Emmons Glacier who requested help through a 911 cell phone call – June

Medical Evacuation of a female climber (30) with a distressed knee injury from the Carbon Glacier – June

Rescue of a guided male client (50) struck by icefall on the Ingraham Glacier – June

Rescue of a male climber (29) with a broken leg on the Emmons Glacier – June

Medical evacuation of a female (15) from Camp Muir suffering from seizures and blackouts – July

Medical evacuation of a male climber (27) suffering a severe diabetic reaction, Kautz Glacier route – July

Medical evacuation of a male climber (34) with altitude related illness, Camp Muir – July

Rescue of a male climber (43) with a broken leg on the Emmons Glacier – July

One less exciting rescue involved the "short-roping" of a solo climber from the summit to Camp Muir in July. This climber chose to ascend despite warnings from guides and other mountaineers. He did not have a solo permit, proper equipment (overnight gear) or preparations (adequate amounts of food and water). Once on the summit, he requested (through other climbing teams) a rescue, stating that he was too tired and hypothermic to descend safely. Climbing rangers from Camp Muir ascended to the Crater Rim and escorted the climber over the course of 11 hours back to Paradise. The climber was cited and convicted in court for endangering the lives of others and soloing without a permit.

Rescues on Mount Ranier are completed by teams, whether they are in the field, in the air, or in the incident command post. Mount Rainier National

Park recognizes and thanks Rainier Mountaineering, Inc. and the Mountain Rescue Association (MRA) for their continued assistance and teamwork in the rescue of persons lost or injured. (Source: Mike Gauthier, Climbing Ranger)

(Editor's Note: This was the information available at the time of publication. If any incident reports that may subsequently be forwarded prove to be informative, they will be included next year.)

(Editor's Note: Last year the Wyoming narratives somehow got dropped from the final manuscript. There were only four climbing accidents in the Tetons in 2002. One narrative is presented below. There was one fatality. Rangers found a solo climber at the base of Symmetry Spire who had obviously fallen, but no other details were evident. The other serious incident was on Nez Perce, in which a belay anchor failure resulted in fractured ribs and a pneumothorax. There were no details as to what caused the anchor to fail.)

FALLING ROCK
Wyoming, Grand Teton National Park, Grand Teton

Around 1900 on July 15, 2002, Teton County Sheriff's Office (TCSO) received a 911 call from Richard Whipple reporting a climbing accident on the North Face of the Grand Teton. The TCSO transferred the call to Teton dispatch, who in turn transferred the call to me. Whipple told me that he was on the North Face about 100 feet below the First Ledge, and that his partner, David James, had been hit by a falling rock and knocked unconscious. James had been unconscious for approximately five minutes but was currently conscious and somewhat oriented. James could not remember the incident. I asked Whipple for his cell number but James could not remember the number. I told Whipple that we would get a rescue in progress and that he should call 911 again in thirty minutes so that we could get further information.

I then contacted dispatch and requested that the contract helicopter be dispatched to the Lupine Meadows Rescue Cache. I also asked dispatch to page the Jenny Lake staff. By radio, I requested that the Jenny Lake staff report to the Rescue Cache prepared for an overnight rescue on the North Face of the Grand Teton. The contract helicopter 2LM arrived at Lupine Meadows at 1921 and shut down. We briefed the pilot and rescuers and then sent Rangers McConnell and Springer for a reconnaissance flight of the accident scene. We also requested a spot weather forecast from Mountain Weather.

The recon flight reported that they had seen the injured party on the North Face below the Guano Chimney. They appeared to be between 600 and 800 feet above the Teton Glacier, in an area exposed to rockfall. Flying conditions at the accident site were very good with calm winds. The decision was made to fly five people and rescue gear to a known landing zone on the glacier. If time allowed and flying conditions remained good, we would insert two rescuers via short-haul onto the North Face. All five rangers were delivered to the glacier and the helicopter was rigged for short-haul. Ranger Byerly was inserted to an area below the accident scene at 2058. Ranger Holm was inserted to the same location at 2104. The helicopter returned to Lupine Meadows and was soon released for the evening. Byerly and Holm began climbing to Whipple, reaching him at approximately 2145. They moved him to a bivy cave for the night.

At 0545, we obtained another weather forecast from Mountain Weather. The forecast called for decent morning conditions, but deteriorating weather in the afternoon. At 0620, I radioed the rescue party. We discussed extrication options. We determined that we would have to move the patient to the previous night's insertion point for either a short-haul extraction or a continued lowering. Byerly and Holm would begin this process while we waited for helicopter 2LM to return to Lupine Meadows at 0830. The various extrication options were discussed at length. We considered extracting the patient, the patient and partner, and all four persons via short-haul. We considered a totally ground-based operation that would require lowering the entire party to the Teton Glacier. We also considered a combination of these techniques, perhaps short-hauling the patient only and the remaining three would self-extricate.

This was a very challenging decision making process. The risks involved with short-haul were weighed against those involved with a lengthy lowering operation. The ever-present possibility of rockfall forced us to judge exposing the helicopter, with a relatively large profile, to danger for a very short period of time vs. exposing the rescue party, with a smaller profile, to danger for a long period of time. An alternate short-haul extraction site was considered, but was abandoned when an episode of rockfall hit the area. At 0807, a second episode of rockfall in the area confirmed that the danger level was high. The rockfall passed through the area that the rescue party would need to descend to the glacier. At 0818, mountain operations chief Springer recommended that given the dangerous rockfall, all four persons be extracted via short-haul. It was confirmed that none of the rockfall occurred in the area in which the helicopter would have to hover to complete an extraction.

Helicopter 2LM arrived at Lupine Meadows at 0845, and Rangers Johnson and Jackson were flown to the accident site for recon. Flying conditions were considered good with calm winds. Particular attention was paid to potential exposure of the aircraft to rockfall during an extraction. A hover power check was performed at the accident site. The rescue party reported that they felt little rotor wash and no ground resonance from the helicopter. The decision was made to extract the patient and his partner in one load via short-haul. Byerly and Holm would then self-extricate from the scene. At 1013, helicopter 2LM left Lupine Meadows en route for short-haul. At this time, more rockfall was witnessed near the rescue party but they confirmed that it would not have threatened the helicopter. The patient and his partner were short-hauled from the rescue site at 1020 and were received by the rescuers on the glacier at 1023. The patient and partner were then loaded inside the aircraft and flown to Lupine Meadows. Medic 1 then transported the patient to St. John's Hospital.

Given the continued rockfall in the descent path of the rescuers, the decision was made to extract Byerly and Holm via short-haul. Byerly and Holm were extracted at 1110 and were down on the Glacier at 1112. All members of the rescue party were then flown from the glacier in two flights and returned to Lupine Meadows. All personnel were back at Lupine Meadows at 1132. A rescue debriefing was concluded at 1300.

(Editor's Note: The lengthy description of the rescue operations is presented so readers can get a sense of the factors that must be taken into consideration and the level of commitment required by the rescuers.

Following next are the narratives from 2003.)

RAPPEL FAILURE/ERROR–NO BACK-UP BELAY AND NO KNOTS ON ENDS OF ROPES
Wyoming, Devils Tower National Monument

On May 17, Jacqueline Weimer (27) sustained fatal injuries after falling approximately 100 meters while rappelling adjacent to the popular El Cracko Diablo climbing route on Devils Tower.

Weimer and her climbing partner had just completed the Soler (5.9) and rejoined three friends in the Meadows, a large ledge system high on the south face of Devils Tower. The group of five decided to rappel together and rigged a double-rope rappel through fixed anchors using 60 meter ropes. A newer, smaller-diameter rope was threaded through the anchors and tied to an older, larger-diameter rope using a Flemish bend. The first person to rappel descended 59 meters—past two sets of intermediate anchors—to a narrow ledge with anchors. Using a different rope, he rigged a single-rope rappel at these anchors and continued down the remaining ten meters to a large ledge. The group planned to descend singly down the double-rope rappel, switching rappels at the small ledge, and then continue down the single-rope rappel, ultimately regrouping at the large ledge. (Although still high-up, this ledge forms the base of Soler and other routes and it is accessed by third class terrain from below.)

While waiting turns to descend the double-rope rappel, each climber observed that the joining knot traveled slightly away from the anchors. Each readjusted the knot before descending. Weimer was the fifth and last person to rappel. At this time her partners were changing shoes and eating lunch at the large ledge below. Weimer reached the intermediate rappel anchors. However, instead of immediately clipping in, she remained in a rappel stance on the two ropes. She then leaned briefly to her right in order to look up and consider how the ropes would pull. At this point her partners watched her fall backward, hit the large ledge, tumble, and continue to fall out of sight. Weimer was found with approximately three meters of excess rope—of the thicker, older rope—running through her rappel device. Presumably, she lost control of the other rope and it slipped through her rappel device.

Analysis

Several factors contributed to this accident, including the extreme length of the rappel, the absence of blocking knots tied at free rope ends, and uneven rope lengths on the double-rope rappel. The compound effect of these factors resulted in a tragic accident.

Choosing to skip two sets of intermediate anchors forced the climbers to rappel dangerously close to the ends of their ropes. Only one to two meters of excess rope are generally available when this same narrow ledge is reached on a double-rope rappel using two standard 60 meter ropes. Nevertheless, many climbers prefer to avoid the hanging stances found at the intermediate sets of anchors and choose to rappel to this same narrow ledge. Although recognizing the length of the rappel, Weimer and her partners still made the conscious decision not to tie blocking knots at the free ends of their ropes because they were concerned that these knots might hang up when the ropes were tossed. Tying, or tossing and then retying, blocking knots can effectively eliminate the risk of rappelling off of rope-ends.

The group intentionally threaded a newer, smaller-diameter (10.2 mm) rope through the anchors and then tied in an older, larger-diameter (10.5 mm) rope, because they felt that doing so would allow for easier rope retrieval. However, this rigging allows the joining knot to travel through—instead of jamming against—the anchors if, on a double-rope rappel, the thinner rope passes through a rappel device slightly faster than the thicker rope. Indeed, while waiting turns to descend the double-rope rappel, each climber observed the joining knot traveling (about 1/2 meter) away from the anchors. Thinner, less worn ropes tend to travel through rappel devices slightly faster than thicker, more worn ropes because slightly less friction is applied to them by the rappel device. This effect can be eliminated if the rappel is rigged in reverse. Larger diameter (or more worn) ropes should be threaded through the anchors and then tied to smaller diameter (or less worn) ropes. In this scenario, instead of traveling, the joining knot will simply jam against the anchor, thereby maintaining even rope lengths.

It is significant that the rope diameters involved in this accident were fairly similar (10.2 vs. 10.5 mm). In this instance it is possible that the differences in sheath wear between the older rope and the brand new rope exaggerated the slight difference in diameter between the two ropes. It is unclear whether the JAWS descending device used by Weimer further exaggerated the situation because of the greater stopping power/friction that this device provides in comparison to other rappel devices. (Source: Chuck Lindsay, Climbing Ranger)

(Editor's Note: Things have changed since 1959, when my partners Carl and Jean Love and I were the 68th–70th to ascend the tower by the only known route. Now there are 6,000–8,000 climbers a year attempting one of the 220 named routes. On this day, there were 82 people on the various routes. Considering that more

than 80,000 climbers have visited the monument, the accident rate is low and there have been very few fatalities, most of them due to rappel errors.)

LIGHTNING, POOR POSITION–LATE START
Wyoming, Grand Teton National Park, Grand Teton

On July 26 at 1535, lightning struck and fatally injured Erica Summers (27) while climbing the Exum Ridge of the Grand Teton. This single lightning strike traveled down the Exum Ridge injuring seven climbers, five seriously. The initial 911 cell phone call at 1546 reported that CPR was in progress, one climber was hanging unresponsive from a rope, multiple people were injured and at least three climbers were unaccounted for.

The response to this incident included two Type-3 interagency contract helicopters with two full helitack crews, one air ambulance, three ground ambulances, and almost all members of the Jenny Lake Sub-District staff. Rangers flown into the Lower Saddle climbed or were short-hauled to two accident scenes. Rangers worked diligently in steep technical terrain to evacuate all the seriously injured patients and the fatality before nightfall.

Analysis

Several members of this group commented about the weather cell that produced the lightning for this incident. What many said was, "It didn't look that bad," or "We've been in way-worse weather." The group had little warning lightning was about to strike. The fatal strike was reportedly the first lightning produced from the storm cell, with no audible thunder as the cell approached. Witnesses reported only one other lightning strike produced from the storm cell, hitting a nearby peak. The characteristic warnings of hair standing up on the back of one's neck or buzzing metal were almost instantaneous with the initial strike. Given the group's position on the mountain, the time of day, and the skill level of those in the group, it is doubtful that had the storm cell approached with thunder 20-40 minutes before hitting the Grand Teton, the group would have been able to move off the mountain fast enough to get to a safer location.

Forecasts and recent weather observations should have indicated to this group that thunderstorms were likely to develop on the afternoon of the 26th. During the two days prior to this incident, afternoon thunderstorms developed and moved over the Tetons. When the initial incident report was broadcast, I looked up into the mountains at a significant storm cell. I wondered if we were going to be able to fly a helicopter at all, and I wondered why these people were on the Exum Ridge at 1546 in the afternoon.

The Exum Ridge is undoubtedly the most popular route on the Grand Teton and thus on a Saturday during the middle of summer, one is bound to encounter other climbers. It is very difficult for a group of 13 people to climb quickly. Getting to the base of Wall Street around 1100 with 13 climbers, many with no climbing experience, would surely have put at least some members of the group near the summit very late in the afternoon, even if other climbing parties had not been encountered.

Fortunately all members of the group wore helmets and their cell phone worked to initiate a rescue response. The group was lucky, however, that a couple of other climbing practices did not result in a greater tragedy. The anchor C. Summers was utilizing at the top of the Friction Pitch was not equalized. All of Rodrigo Liberal's (27) weight and much of Clinton Summers' (27) weight relied on a single .75 Camalot after the strike. Given Team 4's anchor failure, had they fallen further and weighted their rope, which was tied to Liberal's harness, the anchor at the top of the Friction Pitch would have sustained a significant force.

Had the lightning strike occurred when Clinton Summers was passing the knot of the middle climber, Erica Summers, it may have resulted in a much longer fall for Liberal. This potential problem could have been mitigated had E. Summers clipped into the anchor at the top of Friction Pitch and Liberal been tied off short prior to passing the knot.

Fortunately a successful rescue was instrumental in saving lives following this lightning strike. Had weather conditions not improved and rescue resources not been so readily available, more life certainly would have been lost. (Source: Brandon Torres, Grand Teton National Park)

(Editor's Note: The front cover for this years ANAM provides a visual glimpse into the complexity of this rescue. For a full story on the rescue, get a copy of the Jackson Hole News and Guide, July 30, 2003. Two quotes summarize the situation and the expertise of pilots and rangers. First, from Ranger Renny Jackson: "It was something you would expect to see back in the old days—horror stories from the Alps." And from 30-year veteran Ranger Tom Kimbrough, "This might be the most spectacular rescue in the history of American mountaineering in terms of numbers of people being extricated and the way the helicopters worked and how fast the boys did it.")

HAPE/HACE
Wyoming, Grand Teton National Park, Grand Teton

On August 8 about 0400, Ranger McPherson contacted Rangers Holm, Larson, and Montopoli at the Lower Saddle hut. On August 7, Dan and Selanta McPherson (25 and 22) had successfully ascended the Grand Teton by the Complete Exum Route and had returned late that day. During the return, Dan became ill, exhibiting symptoms of High Altitude Pulmonary Edema (HAPE) and possibly High Altitude Cerebral Edema (HACE). He had been unable to sleep and was experiencing violent coughing episodes that resulted in spitting out sputum containing pink phlegm especially after he had lain in a horizontal position. His past medical history included three previous bouts of HACE at altitudes above 14,000 feet, but none was as intense as he was currently experiencing.

Ranger Holm medically evaluated Dan McPherson and made a decision to await daylight hours to escort him down the dangerous terrain to the valley floor. He was instructed to rest in a sitting position and to inform the rangers immediately if his medical condition deteriorated. At 0600 Ranger

Montopoli contacted McPherson and they began to prepare for the descent. His condition had not changed during the night. After Holm reevaluated him medically about 0700, the McPhersons began their descent to the valley floor. Ranger Montopoli escorted them and assisted them by carrying about 20-25 pounds of their equipment.

During the descent, Dan McPherson's condition did not improve. He required several breaks, especially after ascending—which is sometimes required on the descent—any distance. Coughing bouts were especially pronounced when he started to hike after the rest stops. When the group reached the Lupine Meadows Parking Area, D. McPherson stated that he would seek further medical assistance at his home in Cedar City, for which he departed immediately. (Source: Ranger George Montopoli)

(Editor's Note: This is an unusual case of high altitude illness because of its severity at moderate elevation.)

FALL ON ROCK, WEATHER
Wyoming, Grand Teton National Park, Grand Teton

On August 31 at 1855, Exum Guide Jim Williams called via cell phone from the Lower Saddle stating that he could hear yells for help coming from the area by the "Eye of the Needle." Williams stated he was willing to hike up to the scene, estimating it would take him approximately 30 minutes to get there. I told Williams I would request a helicopter so that Rangers could be flown up to the Lower Saddle in the event that Williams encountered injured climbers.

At 1925 Williams was able to talk to Beth Hestick (48) while climbing to the scene. She said that her husband Joe Hestick (47) fell 30 to 60 feet just below the "Eye of the Needle," possibly dislocating his hip. He reportedly was unable to stand and was in significant pain. Williams relayed this information via cell phone and reported he was about 15 minutes from the scene.

By 1932, the helicopter landed at Lupine Meadows and rigged a short-haul with Ranger Scott Guenther as spotter. At 2007 Ranger Vidak was inserted at the scene and began assessing Joe Hestick with help from Williams. At 2019, Ranger Vidak and Joe Hestick were extricated and brought to Lupine Meadows, where Hestick was packaged carefully for ambulance transport to the hospital. (Source: Brandon Torres, Grand Teton National Park)

Analysis

On September 2, after flying Beth Hestick, who had frostbite on both feet, from the Lower Saddle to Lupine Meadows, she told me the following about their accident.

They set out to climb the Grand Teton from their campsite on the Lower Saddle at 0515 on August 29. They intended to climb the Upper Exum route. On the climb, they passed through the feature known as the Eye of the Needle. The Hesticks joined the Exum Ridge at Wall Street and continued the climb. There were two other parties climbing near them for part of the day. As the Hesticks reached the Friction Pitch area, they could see the weather starting to build. They continued climbing, and as they reached the V Pitch, they saw the party ahead of them just finishing the pitch. There were no other parties below the Hesticks. Joe led the V Pitch and Beth followed. The weather was worsening significantly now and they made the decision to descend as soon as possible. Beth led the next short pitch and said that she really knew it was snowing when she put her hand in fresh snow as she continued her lead.

The Hesticks understood from their route description that they could bail from their climb after "crossing a knife edge ridge above the V Pitch." Joe proceeded to lower Beth into various gullies to locate the descent. Each gully seemed to disappear into "oblivion" and Beth would climb back out. The weather had turned extreme by this time with cold temperatures, heavy snow, and clouds. Visibility was very poor and the Hesticks would have had little chance of seeing any landmarks to indicate the descent route.

The Hesticks wisely decided to seek shelter and found a protected cave. They were able to stay dry inside this cave and spent a chilly first night out as the storm continued. They had extra clothes including rain shells, though they did not have rain pants. The storm continued all the next day, and the Hesticks were forced to stay in their cave for a second night. Beth said that this night was much colder. On the morning of their third day, Beth said that the sun came out and they could see where they were. The peak was covered in snow, which was drifted thigh-high in places. The Hesticks decided to climb the final 40 feet to the summit to get their bearings for the descent. They eventually found their way to the double rappel that gets climbing parties down to the Upper Saddle. When they were nearing the end of the technical part of their descent, they could see the Lower Saddle. Joe remarked that he could see their tent and that it was still standing despite the storm. Beth told me that just then she could feel her energy drain away. She knew that they had one short technical section of climbing left to do (the Eye of the Needle) and she kept thinking that accidents happen when you get close to home. Beth found a rappel anchor that would get her past the Eye of the Needle and she decided to rappel. Joe later stated that the only reason he did not do the rappel was because he didn't want to hike back up to Beth and put on his harness.

Joe climbed through the Eye of the Needle while Beth rappelled. At some point he yelled to Beth to ask if she thought he was going the right way. She indicated yes and continued to pull the rappel rope. Beth then heard what she thought was rockfall, but it was really Joe falling. Beth went to Joe and yelled for help toward the Lower Saddle.

The Hesticks were caught in a very severe storm not typical at that time of year. They were well prepared for their climb and had good route information. When they were trapped by the cold, snowy weather, they remained calm and showed good judgment. Joe fell near the end of a huge ordeal. He slipped and fell in an area that he felt he could down-climb. Though I am sure that Joe was physically and psychologically drained, I cannot find fault in his judgment. (Source: Ranger Scott Guenther)

(Editor's Note: While the Hesticks were retreating, another party was attempting to climb the Owen-Spalding route. They chose to continue to the summit, and by the time they returned to the hut at the Lower Saddle at 2100 on September 1, they were wet and cold, especially a 16-year-old who was wearing only cut-off jeans under rain-soaked pants.

Also from this season, there were two fatalities resulting from hikers who got into climbing situations. The first was in June, when Nicole Bloom (23) and her partner became separated around 1100 while on their trip to Garnet Canyon. Weather conditions deteriorated to rain and snow for three hours in the afternoon. A search involving 36 technical climbers found Bloom's body below the south face of the East Ridge of Middle Teton at 1710. She evidently had climbed the Middle Teton Glacier on the north side of the ridge, and as she was trying to downclimb the face in order to rejoin her partner in the South Fork of Garnet Canyon, she fell about 700 feet and died from her head injuries. Bloom was an experienced climber, but during this hike, she evidently made a spontaneous decision to traverse the ridge, and this led her into technical terrain.

In July, a GTNP employee, Lori Sievers (23), went on a hike up to Hanging Canyon, but missed the trail and went around Jenny Lake instead. Rangers think she went over to look at Cube Point from Arrowhead Pool, as she was planning to climb a route on Cube the next week. After looking at the route, she may have looked down in Cascade Canyon and decided to climb down to the trail. It looks like an easy gully; however, once you get down three quarters of the way, it starts to overhang and gets "cliffed out." It appears she fell while attempting to down-climb the last 250 feet to the base of the cliffs.)

STATISTICAL TABLES

TABLE I
REPORTED MOUNTAINEERING ACCIDENTS

	Number of Accidents Reported		Total Persons Involved		Injured		Fatalities	
	USA	CAN	USA	CAN	USA	CAN	USA	CAN
1951	15		22		11		3	
1952	31		35		17		13	
1953	24		27		12		12	
1954	31		41		31		8	
1955	34		39		28		6	
1956	46		72		54		13	
1957	45		53		28		18	
1958	32		39		23		11	
1959	42	2	56	2	31	0	19	2
1960	47	4	64	12	37	8	19	4
1961	49	9	61	14	45	10	14	4
1962	71	1	90	1	64	0	19	1
1963	68	11	79	12	47	10	19	2
1964	53	11	65	16	44	10	14	3
1965	72	0	90	0	59	0	21	0
1966	67	7	80	9	52	6	16	3
1967	74	10	110	14	63	7	33	5
1968	70	13	87	19	43	12	27	5
1969	94	11	125	17	66	9	29	2
1970	129	11	174	11	88	5	15	5
1971	110	17	138	29	76	11	31	7
1972	141	29	184	42	98	17	49	13
1973	108	6	131	6	85	4	36	2
1974	96	7	177	50	75	1	26	5
1975	78	7	158	22	66	8	19	2
1976	137	16	303	31	210	9	53	6
1977	121	30	277	49	106	21	32	11
1978	118	17	221	19	85	6	42	10
1979	100	36	137	54	83	17	40	19
1980	191	29	295	85	124	26	33	8
1981	97	43	223	119	80	39	39	6
1982	140	48	305	126	120	43	24	14
1983	187	29	442	76	169	26	37	7
1984	182	26	459	63	174	15	26	6
1985	195	27	403	62	190	22	17	3
1986	203	31	406	80	182	25	37	14
1987	192	25	377	79	140	23	32	9

	Number of Accidents Reported		Total Persons Involved		Injured		Fatalities	
	USA	CAN	USA	CAN	USA	CAN	USA	CAN
1988	156	18	288	44	155	18	24	4
1989	141	18	272	36	124	11	17	9
1990	136	25	245	50	125	24	24	4
1991	169	20	302	66	147	11	18	6
1992	175	17	351	45	144	11	43	6
1993	132	27	274	50	121	17	21	1
1994	158	25	335	58	131	25	27	5
1995	168	24	353	50	134	18	37	7
1996	139	28	261	59	100	16	31	6
1997	158	35	323	87	148	24	31	13
1998	138	24	281	55	138	18	20	1
1999	123	29	248	69	91	20	17	10
2000	150	23	301	36	121	23	24	7
2001	150	22	276	47	138	14	16	2
2002	139	27	295	29	105	23	34	6
2003	118	29	231	32	105	22	18	6
TOTALS	5840	904	10,681	1,932	4,933	685	1,304	271

(Editor's Note: The totals for these columns have been incorrect from 1981. The individual years have been correct, but the totals went awry, resulting in an understatement of from four to over 300, except for total fatalities in Canada, the total of which was overstated by nine. The totals are now corrected. However, if the totals for Table II were added, they would not jibe with this table either. Vexatious, maybe irrelevant. But we'll try to fix it by the next issue.)

TABLE II

Geographical Districts	1951–2002			2003		
	Number of Accidents	Deaths	Total Persons Involved	Number of Accidents	Deaths	Total Persons Involved
Canada						
Alberta	468	130	998	22	4	26
British Columbia	293	108	621	6	2	6
Yukon Territory	34	26	75	0	0	0
New Brunswick	0	0	0	1	0	0
Ontario	37	9	67	0	0	0
Quebec	28	9	60	1	0	0
East Arctic	8	2	21	0	0	0
West Arctic	1	1	2	0	0	0
Practice Cliffs[1]	20	2	36	0	0	0
United States						
Alaska	447	171	743	14	2	23
Arizona, Nevada Texas	78	16	145	1	0	1
Atlantic–North	855	140	1493	29	1	50
Atlantic–South	86	23	153	1	0	1
California	1,134	269	2,331	39	5	72
Central	131	16	211	1	0	1
Colorado	707	196	2236	4	1	10
Montana, Idaho South Dakota	76	30	120	1	0	2
Oregon	173	99	404	6	3	14
Utah, New Mexico	141	53	264	1	0	1
Washington	983	303	796	11	2	20
Wyoming	519	117	962	10	4	35

[1]This category includes bouldering, artificial climbing walls, buildings, and so forth. These are also added to the count of each province, but not to the total count, though that error has been made in previous years. The Practice Cliffs category has been removed from the U.S. data.

TABLE III

	1951–02 USA	1959–02 CAN.	2003 USA	2003 CAN.
Terrain				
Rock	4053	490	88	13
Snow	2262	339	27	2
Ice	228	133	3	13
River	14	3	0	0
Unknown	22	8	0	1
Ascent or Descent				
Ascent	2657	533	78	22
Descent	2112	347	40	5
Unknown	247	8	0	2
Other [N.B.]	6	0	0	0
Immediate Cause				
Fall or slip on rock	2841	263	46	10
Slip on snow or ice	904	192	11	6
Falling rock, ice, or object	574	126	11	5
Exceeding abilities	489	29	11	0
Avalanche	275	118	1	2
Exposure	251	13	6	0
Illness1	342	24	15	1
Stranded	305	47	5	2
Rappel Failure/Error[2]	252	44	14	0
Loss of control/glissade	184	16	1	0
Fall into crevasse/moat	152	46	0	2
Nut/chock pulled out	174	5	9	3
Failure to follow route	158	29	6	0
Piton/ice screw pulled out	87	12	0	0
Faulty use of crampons	83	5	4	0
Lightning	44	7	1	0
Skiing[3]	50	10	0	0
Ascending too fast	60	0	1	0
Equipment failure	13	3	0	0
Other[4]	332	33	26	1
Unknown	60	8	1	1
Contributory Causes				
Climbing unroped	949	158	11	3
Exceeding abilities	871	199	6	0
Placed no/inadequate protection	625	92	21	2
Inadequate equipment/clothing	619	68	11	0
Weather	434	61	8	2
Climbing alone	362	64	8	3
No hard hat	296	28	8	0
Nut/chock pulled out	196	19	0	6

	1951–01 USA	1959–01 CAN.	2002 USA	2002 CAN.
Contributory Causes, cont.				
Inadequate belay	171	25	10	2
Darkness	132	19	2	1
Poor position	147	20	4	0
Party separated	109	10	1	0
Piton/ice screw pulled out	85	12	1	1
Failure to test holds	88	26	1	2
Exposure	56	13	1	0
Failed to follow directions	70	11	1	0
Illness1	39	9	0	0
Equipment failure	11	7	0	0
Other[4]	248	98	3	1
Age of Individuals				
Under 15	122	12	1	0
15-20	1219	201	7	1
21-25	1283	240	21	6
26-30	1170	201	38	4
31-35	1000	108	11	2
36-50	1046	134	44	2
Over 50	181	24	10	3
Unknown	1867	494	33	10
Experience Level				
None/Little	1635	294	41	0
Moderate (1 to 3 years)	1460	354	34	0
Experienced	1659	419	59	8
Unknown	1881	490	34	21
Month of Year				
January	201	20	1	3
February	193	47	3	4
March	276	66	3	0
April	376	33	5	0
May	829	53	18	2
June	959	64	20	1
July	1037	240	24	4
August	971	171	16	6
September	1124	68	12	2
October	400	34	15	4
November	174	13	1	1
December	86	23	0	1
Unknown	17	1	0	0
Type of Injury/Illness (Data since 1984)				
Fracture	995	195	54	11
Laceration	602	67	22	4
Abrasion	288	74	11	1

	1951–01 USA	1959–01 CAN.	2002 USA	2002 CAN.
Type of Injury/Illness (Data since 1984), cont.				
Bruise	377	76	29	1
Sprain/strain	269	27	12	2
Concussion	196	24	5	4
Hypothermia	138	15	6	0
Frostbite	106	9	6	0
Dislocation	95	12	4	3
Puncture	39	11	3	2
Acute Mountain Sickness	37	0	2	0
HAPE	63	0	2	0
HACE	21	0	2	0
Other[5]	258	43	16	0
None	176	179	8	3

N.B. Some accidents happen when climbers are at the top or bottom of a route, not climbing. They may be setting up a belay or rappel or are just not anchored when they fall. (This category created in 2001 to replace "unknown.")

[1] These illnesses/injuries, which led directly or indirectly to the accident, included: dehydration and exhaustion (6), fatigue (1), HAPE, HACE (4), AMS (3), colitis, back strain.

[2] These include no back-up-knot—so rappelled off end of ropes, inadequate anchors, rope too short, improper use of descending device, improper technique (military "butterfly" rappel) by someone with no experience.

[3] This category was set up originally for ski mountaineering. Backcountry touring or snowshoeing incidents—even if one gets avalanched—are not in the data.

[4] These include: dislodged rocks (11); handhold broke off (3); frostbite (3); unable to self-arrest; late start, route crowded, party too large; lowered off end of top-roped belay; poor leadership, impatience; ankle sprain; knee—medial and lateral ligaments; party separated—inadequate wands for others to follow; partner inadvertently unclipped from protection on ledge.

[5] These included: dehydration and exhaustion (6), colitis, knee—medial and lateral ligaments, back strain, lightning burns (5), pneumothorax, and lacerated liver.

(Editor's Note: Under the category "other," many of the particular items will have been recorded under a general category. For example, the climber who dislodges a rock that falls on another climber would be coded as Falling Rock/Object, or the climber who has a hand hold come loose and falls would also be coded as Fall On Rock.

There was an accident in Alaska on the Devil's Thumb, outside the village of Petersburg, but no details are known as to the cause, so it is reported as "unknown." The two experienced climbers from Vancouver are presumed dead.)

MOUNTAIN RESCUE UNITS IN NORTH AMERICA

**Denotes team fully certified—Technical Rock,
Snow & Ice, Wilderness Search;
S, R, SI = certified partially in Search, Rock, and/or Snow & Ice

ALASKA

Alaska Mountain Rescue Group. PO Box 241102, Anchorage,
AK 99524. www.amrg.org

Denali National Park SAR. PO Box 588, Talkeetna, AK 99676.
Dena_talkeetna@nps.gov

US Army Alaskan Warfare Training Center. #2900 501 Second St., APO AP
96508

ARIZONA

Apache Rescue Team. PO Box 100, St. Johns, AZ 85936

Arizona Department Of Public Safety Air Rescue. Phoenix, Flagstaff, Tucson,
Kingman, AZ

Arizona Division Of Emergency Services. Phoenix, AZ

Grand Canyon National Park Rescue Team. PO Box 129, Grand Canyon, AZ 86023

****Central Arizona Mountain Rescue Team/Maricopa County Sheriff's Office
MR.** PO Box 4004 Phoenix, AZ 85030. www.mcsomr.org

Sedona Fire District Special Operations Rescue Team. 2860 Southwest Dr.,
Sedona, AZ 86336. ropes@sedona.net

****Southern Arizona Rescue Assn/ Pima County Sheriff's Office.** PO Box 12892,
Tucson, AZ 85732. http://hambox.theriver.com/sarci/sara01.html

CALIFORNIA

****Altadena Mountain Rescue Team.** 780 E. Altadena Dr., Altadena, CA 91001
www.altadenasheriffs.org/rescue/amrt.html

****Bay Area Mountain Rescue Team.** PO Box 19184, Stanford, CA 94309
bamru@hooked.net

California Office Of Emergency Services. 2800 Meadowview Rd., Sacramento,
CA. 95832. warning.center@oes.ca.gov

****China Lake Mountain Rescue Group.** PO Box 2037, Ridgecrest, CA 93556
www.clmrg.org

****Inyo County Sheriff's Posse SAR.** PO Box 982, Bishop, CA 93514
inyocosar@juno.com

Joshua Tree National Park SAR. 74485 National Monument Drive,
Twenty Nine Palms, CA 92277. patrick_suddath@nps.gov

****Los Padres SAR Team.** PO Box 6602, Santa Barbara, CA 93160-6602

****Malibu Mountain Rescue Team.** PO Box 222, Malibu, CA 90265.
www.mmrt.org

****Montrose SAR Team.** PO Box 404, Montrose, CA 91021

****Riverside Mountain Rescue Unit.** PO Box 5444, Riverside,
CA 92517. www.rmru.org   rmru@bigfoot.com

San Bernardino County Sheriff's Cave Rescue Team. 655 E. Third St.
San Bernardino, CA 92415
www.sbsd-vfu.org/units/SAR/SAR203/sar203_1.htm

****San Bernardino County So/ West Valley SAR.** 13843 Peyton Dr., Chino Hills,
CA 91709.

San Diego Mountain Rescue Team. PO Box 81602, San Diego, CA 92138. www.sdmrt.org

San Dimas Mountain Rescue Team. PO Box 35, San Dimas, CA 91773

Santa Clarita Valley SAR / L.A.S.O. 23740 Magic Mountain Parkway, Valencia, CA 91355. http://members.tripod.com/scvrescue/

Sequoia-Kings Canyon National Park Rescue Team. Three Rivers, CA 93271

Sierra Madre SAR. PO Box 24, Sierra Madre, CA 91025. www.mra.org/smsrt.html

Ventura County SAR. 2101 E. Olson Rd, Thousand Oaks, CA 91362 www.vcsar.org

Yosemite National Park Rescue Team. PO Box 577-SAR, Yosemite National Park, CA 95389

COLORADO

Alpine Rescue Team. PO Box 934, Evergreen, CO 80439 www.heart-beat-of-evergreen.com/alpine/alpine.html

Colorado Ground SAR. 2391 Ash St, Denver, CO 80222 www.coloradowingcap.org/CGSART/Default.htm

Crested Butte SAR. PO Box 485, Crested Butte, CO 81224

DOUGLAS COUNTY SEARCH AND RESCUE. PO Box 1102, Castle Rock, CO 80104. www.dcsarco.org info@dcsarco.org

El Paso County SAR. 3950 Interpark Dr, Colorado Springs, CO 80907-9028. www.epcsar.org

Eldorado Canyon State Park. PO Box B, Eldorado Springs, CO 80025

Grand County SAR. Box 172, Winter Park, CO 80482

Larimer County SAR. 1303 N. Shields St., Fort Collins, CO 80524. www. fortnet.org/LCSAR/ lcsar@co.larimer.co.us

Mountain Rescue Aspen. 630 W. Main St, Aspen, CO 81611 www.mountainrescueaspen.org

Park County SAR, CO. PO Box 721, Fairplay, CO 80440

Rocky Mountain National Park Rescue Team. Estes Park, CO 80517

Rocky Mountain Rescue Group. PO Box Y, Boulder, CO 80306 www.colorado.edu/StudentGroups/rmrg/ rmrg@colorado.edu

Routt County SAR. PO Box 772837, Steamboat Springs, CO 80477 RCSAR@co.routt.co.us

Summit County Rescue Group. PO Box 1794, Breckenridge, CO 80424

Vail Mountain Rescue Group. PO Box 1597, Vail, CO 81658 http://sites.netscape.net/vailmra/homepage vmrg@vail.net

Western State College Mountain Rescue Team. Western State College Union, Gunnison, CO 81231. org_mrt@western.edu

IDAHO

Bonneville County SAR. 605 N. Capital Ave, Idaho Falls, ID 83402 www.srv.net/~jrcase/bcsar.html

Idaho Mountain SAR. PO Box 741, Boise, ID 83701. www.imsaru.org rsksearch@aol.com

MAINE

Acadia National Park SAR. Bar Harbor, Maine

MARYLAND
Maryland SAR Group. 5434 Vantage Point Road, Columbia, MD 21044
Peter_McCabe@Ed.gov

MONTANA
Glacier National Park SAR. PO Box 423, Glacier National Park,
West Glacier, MT 59936
Northwest Montana Regional SAR Assn. c/o Flat County SO,
800 S. Main, Kalispell, MT 59901
Western Montana Mountain Rescue Team. University of Montana,
University Center—Rm 105 Missoula, MT 59812

NEVADA
Las Vegas Metro PD SAR. 4810 Las Vegas Blvd., South Las Vegas,
NV 89119. www.lvmpdsar.com

NEW MEXICO
Albuquerque Mountain Rescue Council. PO Box 53396, Albuquerque,
NM 87153. www.abq.com/amrc/ albrescu@swcp.com

NEW HAMPSHIRE
Appalachian Mountain Club. Pinkham Notch Camp, Gorham, NH 03581
Mountain Rescue Service. PO Box 494, North Conway, NH 03860

NEW YORK
76 SAR. 243 Old Quarry Rd., Feura Bush, NY 12067
NY State Forest Rangers. 50 Wolf Rd., Room 440C, Albany, NY 12233

OREGON
Corvallis Mountain Rescue Unit. PO Box 116, Corvallis, OR 97339
www.cmrv.peak.org
(S, R) **Deschutes County SAR.** 63333 West Highway 20, Bend, OR 97701
Eugene Mountain Rescue. PO Box 20, Eugene, OR 97440
Hood River Crag Rats Rescue Team. 2880 Thomsen Rd., Hood River,
OR 97031
Portland Mountain Rescue. PO Box 5391, Portland, OR 97228
www.pmru.org info@pmru.org

PENNSYLVANNIA
Allegheny Mountain Rescue Group. c/o Mercy Hospital,
1400 Locust, Pittsburgh, PA 15219. www.asrc.net/amrg
Wilderness Emergency Strike Team. 11 North Duke Street, Lancaster,
PA 17602. www.west610.org

UTAH
Davis County Sheriff's SAR. PO Box 800, Farmington, UT 84025
www.dcsar.org
Rocky Mountain Rescue Dogs. 3353 S. Main #122, Salt Lake City, UT 84115
Salt Lake County Sheriff's SAR. 4474 South Main St., Murray, UT 84107

San Juan County Emergency Services. PO Box 9, Monticello, UT 84539
**Utah County Sherrif's SAR. PO Box 330, Provo, UT 84603. ucsar@utah.
uswest.net
**Weber County Sheriff's Mountain Rescue. 745 Nancy Dr, Ogden,
UT 84403. http://planet.weber.edu/mru
Zion National Park SAR. Springdale, UT 84767

VERMONT
**Stowe Hazardous Terrain Evacuation. P.O. Box 291, Stowe, VT 05672
www.stowevt.org/htt/

VIRGINIA
Air Force Rescue Coordination Center. Suite 101, 205 Dodd Building,
Langley AFB, VA 23665. www2.acc.af.mil/afrcc/airforce.rescue@usa.net

WASHINGTON STATE
**Bellingham Mountain Rescue Council. PO Box 292, Bellingham, WA 98225
**Central Washington Mountain Rescue Council. PO Box 2663, Yakima,
WA 98907. www.nwinfo.net/~cwmr/ cwmr@nwinfo.net
**Everett Mountain Rescue Unit. PO Box 2566, Everett, WA 98203
emrui@aol.com
Mount Rainier National Park Rescue Team. Longmire, WA 98397
North Cascades National Park Rescue Team. 728 Ranger Station Rd,
Marblemount, WA 98267
**Olympic Mountain Rescue. PO Box 4244, Bremerton, WA 98312
www.olympicmountainrescue.org information@olympicmountainrescue.org
Olympic National Park Rescue Team. 600 Park Ave, Port Angeles, WA 98362
**Seattle Mountain Rescue. PO Box 67, Seattle, WA 98111
www.eskimo.com/~pc22/SMR/smr.html
**Skagit Mountain Rescue. PO Box 2, Mt. Vernon, WA 98273
**Tacoma Mountain Rescue. PO Box 696, Tacoma, WA 98401
www.tmru.org
North Country Volcano Rescue Team. 404 S. Parcel Ave, Yacolt, WA 98675
www.northcountryems.org/vrt/index.html

WASHINGTON, DC
National Park Service, EMS/SAR Division. Washington, DC
US Park Police Aviation. Washington, DC

WYOMING
Grand Teton National Park Rescue Team. PO Box 67, Moose, WY 83012
Park County SAR, WY. Park County SO, 1131 11th, Cody, WY 82412

CANADA
North Shore Rescue Team. 147 E. 14th St, North Vancouver, B.C.,
Canada V7L 2N4
**Rocky Mountain House SAR. Box 1888, Rocky Mountain House, Alberta,
Canada T0M 1T0

MOUNTAIN RESCUE ASSOCIATION

c/o PO Box 501
Poway, CA 92074 USA
www.mra.org

Dan Hourihan, President/CEO
Alaska Mountain Rescue Group, AK
danh@dnr.state.ak.us
907-269-8698

Monty Bell, Vice President/Membership
San Diego Mountain Rescue Unit, CA
mbell@newwaypro.com
858-505-8300 x310

Kayley Trujillo, Secretary-Treasurer/CFO
San Diego Mountain Rescue Unit, CA
kayley@kayley.net

Fran Martoglio, Member At Large
Tacoma Mountain Rescue Unit, WA
thegirlpilot@hotmail.com

Neil Van Dyke, Member at Large
Stowe Hazardous Terrain Evacuation, VT
neilvd@stoweagle.com

Tim Kovacs, Public Affairs Director/ PIO, Past President
Central AZ Mountain Rescue/Maricopa County SO MR, AZ
tkovacs@mindspring.com
602-819-4066

Charley Shimanski, Education Director/PIO
Alpine Rescue Team, CO
cshiman@americanalpineclub.org
303-384-0110 x11

Dr. Ken Zafren, MD, FACEP, Medical Chair
Alaska Mountain Rescue Group, AK
zafren@alaska.net